Collecting & Display

Collecting

& Display

Alistair McAlpine
and Cathy Giangrande

conran
OCTOPUS

*To my brothers William and David McAlpine,
both imaginative collectors.* RAMcA

*In memory of my father George, and for my mother
Irene, to whom I owe my wings.* CG

First published in 1998 by
Conran Octopus Limited
37 Shelton Street
London WC2H 9HN

ISBN 1 85029 956 0

Commissioning Editor Denny Hemming
Managing Editor Kate Bell
Editorial Assistant Tanya Robinson
Copy Editors Phyllis Richardson, Caroline Fraser Ker

Design Ninety Seven Plus Ltd
Stylists for Special Photography Pep Sala, Cynthia Inions

Picture Research Jo Alexander
Production Julian Deeming
Index Helen Baz

British Library Cataloguing-in-Publication Data.
A catalogue record for this book is available from
the British Library.

Printed and bound in China.

*Previous pages: These sensuous undulating forms belong to a
collection of green glazed ceramic* hu, *or Chinese ceremonial vessels, from the Eastern Han period. Originally filled with offerings of
meat, grain or wine, they were buried with the occupants of tombs.*

*Right: Set against an inspiring city skyline, these elegant glass
vases, arranged in blocks of similar hues, echo the towering
sequence of buildings behind. Like the buildings, they are a testa-
ment to man's ability to create objects of great strength and beauty.*

Contents

Preface

Amongst collectors and dealers in works of art and objects of curiosity, there is a term normally referred to as 'the eye'. In common language, having a brilliant eye means that you are able to spot the special quality of an object or painting long before it becomes popular. Those who have an eye create taste, often buying and even selling objects long before those objects are considered works of art. As often as not, these people have either sold their collection or died before the value of its contents has been recognized. To be a pioneer in the world of avant-garde art is a lonely business. With collecting, however, it is entirely different: no matter how obscure the category of object that you choose to collect, the act of collecting brings you into contact with other people.

All my life I have collected one thing or another, from apparently humble stones to paintings as rarefied as the works of Jackson Pollock and Mark Rothko. Out of collecting have risen some of my longest and deepest friendships. When you collect rare breeds of chickens or varieties of snowdrops, you make the most unusual friends. As for 'the eye', this is not such an uncommon commodity. Anyone who collects with passion, expresses their own views with conviction and backs those views with their energy and financial resources, can be said to have 'the eye'.

Opposite: *New additions do not always find their place alongside the rest of the collection straight away. Frequently a collector will require time for reflection before being seduced by an object's form, grace or colour. The collector's artistic skill will then come into play to find the best setting for each piece.*

In the days when I first collected paintings by the Abstract Expressionists and Colour-field painters of the New York school, visitors to my home, without the slightest hesitation, and without the benefit of an invitation, would offer their opinions on my collection. They could not understand how I could possibly live with such 'things' hanging on my walls. To them, I may as well have been exhibiting lewd art or dead animals. Today, however, many of those who passed those remarks swoon over the work of artists who exhibit lewd art or dead animals suspended in formaldehyde. It is only a matter of taste, whether you are creating taste or following taste.

In this book, my co-author Cathy Giangrande and I have tried to show what diverse objects have been collected over the years – from fine art to natural curiosities and ephemera – and how collectors have displayed these collections with imagination and style. Along the way we have looked at thousands of photographs and visited many collections, coming to the firm conclusion that it is passion, enthusiasm and a capacity to enjoy the thrill of collecting, that makes the ownership of such objects worthwhile.

ALISTAIR McALPINE

The Cabinet of Curiosities

THE ORIGINS OF COLLECTING are almost as old as mankind. When primitive man collected pebbles for their shape or colour these represented his earliest attempts to gather objects for intellectual and spiritual reasons. Such symbolic objects were displayed by being worn in life and in death. In some ancient cultures a hole in the centre of a stone related to the sun or the moon, or an unusual formation in the grain could give the impression of a human eye, and both were possibly talismans. As man learned how to work precious metal into weapons and ornaments, these too became prized possessions, also eventually destined for burial mounds. It was not long, however, before collected treasures were placed in sacred repositories to inspire the living as well as the dead.

War and worship were the primary inspirations for the first collections. As the famous temples of Delphi and Delos show, the Greeks, too, buried people with valuable items, such as bronze fibulae, pins and figurines, as public dedications to their gods. Some temples became like war museums and served as armouries stocked with arms and armour acquired from defeated enemies and personal offerings from grateful victors. Sometimes the temples themselves were built with the proceeds of successful campaigns so that collections became linked not only with the gods, but with the spoils of war.

Popular collecting, however, appears to have begun after Greek unification in the fourth century BC, when objects from the East, especially Persia, made their way into homes in Hellenistic Greece. Wall hangings, carved jewels, cameos and secular wall paintings, even painted and carved portraits became fashionable and an art market developed in which signed works by an important artist were valued. By the start of the Roman Empire under Augustus (27 BC) a true collecting frenzy had emerged in both the private and public realms. There were public collections scattered throughout the Roman Empire containing works of mostly Greek origin – paintings, marble and gold statues, masks and bronze shields. Many, like the Forum of Augustus and the Forum of Trojan were similar to the national galleries of today.

Opposite: Cabinets made from rare woods embellished with ivory, ebony or pietra dura *were produced by Renaissance craftsmen for the display of precious possessions. This antique giltwood 'cabinet of curiosities', with its multiplicity of pigeonholes, makes a perfect setting for all kinds of diminutive objects, from rare Fabergé eggs to more prosaic artefacts.*

The private collectors accumulated objects much like those found in the public temples, purchasing their items at the Villa Publica in Rome from the antique dealers of the day who sold sculptures, paintings, silver, carpets, books and gems to the wealthy, and fossils and natural curiosities to the more modest collectors. The growing market also attracted unscrupulous dealers who encouraged thievery and instituted the production of forgeries.

In Japan and China collecting was at first the luxury of rulers and nobles, and these collections changed hands with successive conquerors. During China's first three dynasties – the Xia, the Shang and the Zhou – the advent of bronze metallurgy allowed the creation of imposing drinking vessels and food containers, used for ritual offerings, that symbolized power and prestige and were often plundered, along with weaponry. Such pieces would be buried along with other goods by fleeing armies only to be uncovered and stolen by the victors. The first Emperor of Qin, who unified China in 221 BC, ordered 'that all the bronze vessel and weapons captured from his vanquished enemies be melted down and made into twelve colossal bronze statues to adorn his palaces'.

In addition to the plunder of warfare, trade also ensured that precious objects no longer stayed with one collector through life and death. Spurred on not only by the pursuit of profits and the allure of the exotic, but also by collectors eager to enhance their own status, trade between the East and West developed from around the first century BC. During the reign of Augustus, trade with the East flourished. The shifting of the empire eastwards to Constantinople in the third century, however, led to the blockading of sea and overland routes so that it was not until the middle of the seventh century, when the three empires – the Tang in China, Islam in the Middle East and the Byzantine in Europe – controlled much of the known world's wealth and commerce, that trade expanded again and the taste for foreign luxuries spread.

Buddhist pilgrims from India and Japan, merchants from the Middle East, traders in gems from Arabia, and envoys from almost all parts of the known world converged at places like the Chinese capital of Changan. In Japan, a storehouse connected to the Todai-ji temple in Nara contains a treasury of Tang and other contemporary objects,

the personal collection amassed by the Emperor Shomu. During the golden age of Tang China, goods were brought to China from India and South-east Asia as well as Iran and the Mediterranean countries. Europeans fell under the spell of Eastern exoticism around the time that China came under Mongol control, 1279, and the famous Venetian trading family Polo travelled to the court of Kublai Khan. They came back with a glowing report of the Khan's private possessions: 'his treasures of gold and silver, precious stones and pearls, his ladies and concubines, all laid out for his comfort and convenience'.

Trading cultures influenced each other not only in what they collected but in how they went about it. Collecting in the European tradition became widespread in China during the late Ming dynasty, assisted by books such as the *Treatise on Superfluous Things* by Wen Zhenheng, which told how to gain status and knowledge by amassing important collections of paintings and calligraphy. It also suggested 'that women who would be social climbers keep parrots, fish, golden pheasants, cocks, and turkeys'. In Japan, under Tokugawa Shogunate in the Edo period (1603–1868), collecting was greatly influenced by China – both artefacts and traditions – and the newly wealthy merchants collected paintings, calligraphy, lacquer and kosodes, short-sleeved kimonos which were worn and changed several times during long kabuki performances, to show off the range of their collection and therefore their wealth.

In Europe, throughout the Middle Ages, most collecting was done not by individuals but by the Church, which kept treasuries of holy artefacts, many made from precious metals and jewels. These great collections were also store-houses for gold and silver, which was melted down and used for currency in times of need, as well as havens for the more curious items, such as dinosaur bones (thought to be bones of a giant), whale skeletons and ivory tusks.

There were, nevertheless, some important private collectors in Europe in the late Middle Ages. Especially notable were the French nobility, and among them Jean, Duc de Berry (1340–1416). He was described by a contemporary as a compulsive collector, ready to sacrifice affairs of state in the hope of acquiring some new and irresistible object. Besides his penchant for items crafted from precious metals and jewels with religious

The pictorial equivalent of a Renaissance nobleman's cabinet, Holbein's The Ambassadors, *painted in 1533, depicts two diplomats: on the left, Jean de Dinteville, the French Ambassador to London, and, on the right, Georges de Selve, the Bishop of Lavour. The men frame a heap of intriguing objects: a celestial globe, two quadrants, a sundial and a torquetum – an astronomical instrument for measuring celestial bodies – on the top shelf; below, a lute with a broken string, a terrestrial globe and an open book. The items are emblematic of a tumultuous period in the history of Western Europe when both Church and State were in crisis. Powerless, the ambassadors can only contemplate the inevitability of death and redemption, as symbolized by the skull in the foreground and the crucifix in the top left-hand corner.*

Painted in 1666 by Georg Hinz, the Kunstkammer Rega *shows a typical princely collection, clearly influenced by the great medieval ecclesiastical treasuries of the thirteenth century. These 'cabinets of wonders' were used to display the wealth of their owners, with pride of place given to virtuoso* objets d'art, *ornamental ivory cups, bejewelled shrines and portrait medallions.*

significance, he also, unlike his contemporaries, collected many of the kinds of objects found in the later *Wunderkammers*, 'rooms of wonder', or cabinets of curiosities, which held collections of art or unusual objects. The Duc de Berry's collection included, among other things, vessels made from coconut shells, carved ivory beads and mounted pieces of oriental porcelain, as well as the amazing illuminated calendar pages of the *Très Riches Heures*.

Among the intellectual pursuits of Enlightenment and the fresh attempts to understand the world, European collectors at the beginning of the sixteenth century sought the rare, exotic and exceptional. The discovery of foreign lands and the quest for new experiences inspired the Renaissance passion for collecting, organizing and displaying wondrous objects both natural and man-made. In Paris,

Venice, Leiden and London, remarkable *Wunderkammers* were assembled. A great variety of people collected at this time, including the Pope, cardinals and clerics, kings and other noblemen and members of the professional classes. The ownership of obscure and rare objects conferred on its owner the status of 'a learned person' involved in the pursuit of knowledge. Often *Wunderkammers* were adjoined by libraries and laboratories to aid in the attempt to unravel the mysteries of the universe through the enlightened skills of science.

The collections were kept in anything from decorative cabinets to small rooms or, in the case of Archduke Ferdinand II, who founded the Ambras *Wunderkammer* at his palace near Innsbruck, 'in a large room with eighteen cupboards, placed back to back...' and filled with his most

Above: *One of two cabinets, thought to date from the 1660s, belonging to the canon of Canterbury Cathedral. His cabinets incorporate coin trays and drawers containing gems, rock samples and even fake antiquities.*

Left: *Renaissance tastes favoured richly ornamented weapons and armour. In this engraving, Charles I, an omnivorous collector, is shown by William Hole with just part of his collection of armour.*

Above: *A depiction of the museum of 'wonderful things' assembled by Olaus Worm, Professor of Natural Philosophy at Copenhagen. In 1655 the collection was acquired by Frederick III and incorporated into the Danish Royal collections.*

Below: *Although there are some* artificialia *to be found in the collection of the pharmacist Ferrante Imperato in Naples (1599), most of the items are animal, plant or mineral in origin and are more specifically scientific, reflecting not only the social status of the collector, but also his intellectual and professional interests.*

prized objects arranged according to a carefully elaborated system drawn from Pliny's *Historia naturalis*. His collection of objects included 'silver-mounted ostrich eggs, rhinoceros horns, seashells, and objects decorated with casts from nature made by Nuremberg's leading silversmith, Wentzel Jamnitzer'. The walls were filled with 'paintings of living anomalies: giants, dwarves, and cripples'.

As well as contributing to the reputations of individuals, the collections brought fame to towns and cities, enticing hoards of curious visitors. In 1556 the Netherlandish collector Hubert Goltzius, in search of antiquities, listed 968 collections located in the Low Countries, Germany, Austria, Switzerland, France and Italy which an interested traveller could visit.

Below: The collection in the grand saloon and gallery at the Leverian Museum, amassed by Sir Ashton Lever, whose interest in ethnography was stimulated by the voyages of exploration which led to increasing curiosity about non-European peoples. His excessive zeal for accumulating objects forced him to sell the collection in 1785.

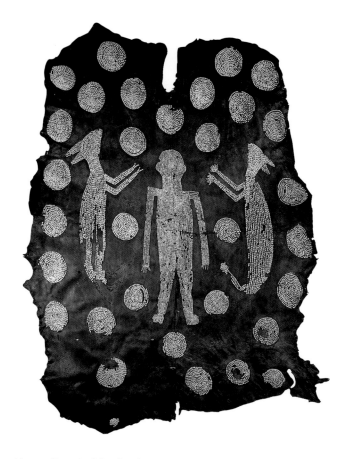

Above: *Captain John Smith was given this magnificent shell-decorated deerskin robe by the Algonquin Chieftain Powhatan, father of Princess Pocahontas, in 1608. Smith later gave the 'mantle' to the Tradescants for their Cabinet of Exotica. In 1683 the contents of the cabinet were acquired for the Ashmolean Museum, Oxford.*

During the Renaissance anything weird, peculiar or distorted was collectable. Andrea Vendramin, a Venetian collector, amassed everything from 'pictures, sculptures of divinities, oracles and ancient idols, costumes of different lands, ancient instruments of sacrifice' to 'pure, mixed and composite natural substances; whelks, shells and conches from various parts of the world' and 'illustrated books on chronology, prints, animals, fish and birds; plants and flowers'. Even more bizarre were the London collections of Walter Cope which, at the end of the sixteenth century, included 'an African charm made of teeth, a felt cloak from Arabia, and shoes from many strange lands', as well as 'the twisted horn of a bull seal. The bauble and bells of Henry VIII's fool. A unicorn's tail. A flying rhinoceros... a narrow Indian canoe'. Whatever was rare, mysterious, curious or unusual was added to produce a microcosm of the world, a mirror of the universe.

In many parts of Europe a greater understanding of the material nature of the world inspired collectors and the frenzy for the curious began to wane. Two of the great English collectors of the seventeenth century, who bridged the gap between the educational and the curious, were John Tradescant the Elder and his son, who put together

Opposite and below: In 1718 Sir Hans Sloane acquired a collection of natural rarities procured by the apothecary James Petiver. Petiver's collections of insects were preserved in two distinct styles. The moths and butterflies (opposite) were pressed and attached by a hinge in an enclosed envelope of mica, enabling the undersides to be examined. The drawers (below) contain beetles preserved in small glass-topped boxes acquired from James Petiver, Joseph Dandridge and Sir Hans Sloane. Dandridge, an insect enthusiast, played a major role in the development of entomology in England.

a cabinet of curiosities for profit and with the aim of transmitting knowledge. The collection included the American Indian chief Powhatan's mantle, a jasper heart, Guy Fawkes's lantern, Henry VII's stirrups, a pair of gloves presented to Elizabeth I, a crystal ball and alabaster panels, along with 'a bracelet made out of the thighs of Indian flies... and a coat made out of the entrails of fishes'. The majority of the items in the collection came from Asia and the Americas, and, like the best collections of this period, it contained an assortment of ethnological specimens. The Tradescants set up their curiosities on the South Bank of the Thames and charged visitors a fee to view them. The crowds of the day were enchanted.

Others were similarly keen to share the wonders of their collections. Sir Hans Sloane, a scientist, physician and antiquarian, was the model of a man in search of wisdom at the end of the seventeenth century. Sloane, along with other scholarly collectors of the time, including Johann Daniel Major, a physician and native of Kiel, and Michael Bernhard Valentini, an experimental scientist and professor of medicine at Giessen University, published encyclopaedic manuals of their collections and research on collecting. Sloane travelled far and wide amassing huge collections of both natural and man-made specimens, along with a vast library. Seashells and beetles, a painting of the Dodo, a giant pair of buffalo horns, drawings of animals and artefacts from distant and exotic parts of the world were all carefully catalogued in 46 folio volumes, 31 of which happily survive in the British Library. As personal physician to the Duke of Albemarle, Governor of Jamaica, Sloane spent 15 months there gathering specimens, publishing his finds as the two-volume *Natural History of Jamaica*, a massive undertaking for its time. Sloane wrote, 'the collection and accurate arrangement of these curiosities constituted my major contribution to the advancement of science'. His life's work and collections helped form the basis for the British Museum.

The drive to amass or record exotic treasures had a new impetus from the middle of the seventeenth century – the Grand Tour. During this time, innumerable members of the European upper classes began travelling through Europe, mainly to Italy, buying fine paintings and sculpture enthusiastically to decorate their manor houses and

Pap. fusco Albo & Rubro maculati.

M.T.315.TAB.4.f.1.2. Engl. Testudo
1384. 85.

CAROL.
1380.k. 152

510
1380. 152

M.PET.327.Tab.2.t.XI. English
admiral. 1380.g. 152

1378.a.86

1380. i.
MARYL. american. 152

Pap. Oculati.

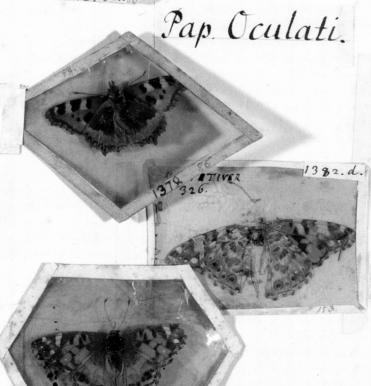

1378. RTIVER 1382.d.
326.
1383. 154
153

1407. 173

Mus. PETIV. 326.
1382.e.153
dr. Martini. Q.N.33.5. American.

firmly establish their social positions. One such enthusiast was Sir John Soane, an architect who built himself a fine residence in Lincoln's Inn Fields and then set about filling it with fragments of architectural detailing, antiquities and fine paintings from his trips to Italy. Another, Sir William Hamilton, became an influential figure in the history of the British Museum, as a result of his stunning collection of Greek vases and collections of artefacts recovered from the early excavations at Pompeii. Thomas Howard, the Earl of Arundel, also scoured Italy in search of Greek and Roman marbles, only to have his vast collection randomly dispersed by his disinterested heirs.

Within Italy itself, the rise of the influential Medicis, and their interest in the collection of art and artefacts, led to a significant change in cultural policy. The Florentine commercial family embarked on a path of collecting and patronage that reflected their strong political aspirations and power as a ruling family. Like many collectors before him, Piero de' Medici stored his celebrated vessels made of semi-precious stones, coins and cameos in a private study where he could contemplate them at his leisure. But when the Grand Duke Francesco de' Medici succeeded his father as Grand Duke of Tuscany in 1574, he transferred the 'secret collections' to the Uffizi Palace, where they

Opposite: *A connoisseur amongst collectors, Sir John Soane transformed his former home in Lincoln's Inn Fields, London, into a museum. The collection includes numerous sculptural fragments and plaster casts, such as those seen here surrounding a bust by Sir Francis Chantrey of Soane himself.*

Above: *The voyages undertaken by Captain James Cook had explicit scientific purposes. On his first expedition in 1768, he set out to observe the transit of Venus, in an attempt to find a means of measuring longitude, but also collected exotic objects from Polynesia and the Northwest Coast of the Americas and Alaska.*

went on public display. As a result, the collection became an acclaimed status symbol, a display of knowledge, an instrument of propaganda and an expression of the worthiness of the individual and his family for high office.

As the end of the eighteenth century approached and more collectors catalogued and published their finds, it was no longer enough merely to amass objects that aroused curiosity. Collectors were expected to note each individual item's place in history or the natural world. From his three voyages of discovery, Captain James Cook returned to Britain with shiploads of exotic artefacts gathered from the South Pacific and the distant continent of Australia. With him travelled the botanist Joseph Banks, who collected natural specimens, such as rocks, minerals, fossils, plants and the skins of birds and mammals, and then organized them according to the recently developed Linnaean system of classification.

At the same time, a similar rationale was also being applied to human remains. Augustus Henry Lane Fox Pitt-Rivers, a legendary figure in the world of archaeology, set about classifying human artefacts using the Darwinian system and produced a typology in archaeology which took into account both spatial and chronological dimensions. He gathered tools, weapons, ritualistic ornaments and domestic objects from all over the world and used them to illustrate the evolutionary development of early man. His collection of over 20,000 objects formed the beginnings of the Pitt-Rivers Museum in Oxford.

Albertus Seba, a German-born apothecary, sold his first, largely ethnographic Wunderkammer *to the Russian Tsar Peter the Great in 1717. His second cabinet of natural rarities, including birds, plants, butterflies, amphibians, fish, shells and fossils, was recorded in a sumptuous catalogue, much admired by Linnaeus.*

Charles Willson Peale, in his self-portrait of 1822, holds back a curtain to reveal collections at his Philadelphia museum, including the giant jaw and tibia of a mastodon with its mounted skeleton, as well as birds, minerals, insects and fossils, displayed in taxonomic order, and busts of heroes from the American Revolution.

A gem of eccentricity, the Pitt-Rivers Museum, Oxford, is crammed to the gunnels with weird ethnographic objects from the known and disappeared world. Here, Inuit rainwear made from walrus intestines rubs shoulders with a witch in a bottle. Collecting examples of closely related objects to illustrate the development of early and primitive man was typical of the period, and remains an essential methodology today.

At the beginning of the nineteenth century, the desire to establish a patterned system into which natural things could fit and to increase knowledge through the arrangement and cataloguing of pieces also affected how modern and classical art collections were being displayed. In parts of Europe, great royal art collections were being exhibited to the public with sculpture and pictures arranged in chronological order. In 1721 Frederick Augustus I, King of Poland, began the refurbishment of his Green Vaults Treasury in Dresden Castle, setting out a suite of seven galleries filled with works from the *Kunstkammer* – so called because the emphasis was on art rather than the natural wonders of the *Wunderkammer* – the silver vaults and his own collections. The public were admitted for one ducat.

Similarly, the royal Viennese collection was rehoused in the Belvedere in 1776, with pictures arranged by art-historical periods and clearly labelled. The private collections of the kings of France were moved to the Galerie d'Apollon at the Louvre around this time and, in 1833, many of the holdings in the Danish *Kunstkammer* were transferred to Rosenborg Palace which was opened to visitors. Carefully organized and catalogued, the public who were allowed in to marvel at the display also acquired knowledge from it.

While the riches of the princely collections in Europe were being organized and opened to view, in America artists, doctors and statesmen were busy amassing a range of items, including prints, books, furniture and natural specimens, with a view to creating public museums. Charles Willson Peale (1741–1827), an artist based in Philadelphia, constructed a gallery to display both his paintings of heroes of the Revolution and cases containing birds, fossils, minerals and insects, arranged according to the Linnaean system. Peale wrote that in 'an extensive

CAMBRIDGE GEOLOGICAL MUSEUM, 1842.

The Woodwardian Museum of Geology, Cambridge, was the first of the university museums of geology. John Woodward's collection of around 9,400 specimens, mainly of rocks, minerals and fossils, was amassed between 1688 and 1724, and, unlike the more usual miscellaneous assemblages of the rare and curious, was a well-documented 'scientific' collection which he used as the basis for elaborate classifications. Founded in 1840, the museum was relocated in 1904 when it became known as the Sedgwick Museum.

collection should be found the various inhabitants of every element, not only of the animal, but also specimens of the vegetable tribe – and all the brilliant and precious stones down to the common grit'. Furthermore, human fossils 'should grace every well stored Museum'.

Peale expected his collections to excite curiosity, to teach, and to induce in the onlooker the desire to learn. Collections such as these were filled with optimism, demonstrating both the complexity and an appreciation of the beauty of the natural world. Peale's Museum, which opened in Philadelphia in 1802, displayed a complete mastodon skeleton surrounded by other curiosities, including tattooed human heads and a five-headed cow, to attract the public. This balance of roles, both as a scientific collection and as a vehicle of popular commercial entertainment, was not easy to maintain, nor was it particularly successful. Upon Peale's death in 1827, the museum was purchased by P. T. Barnum and Peale's educational vision was quickly swallowed up by Barnum's desire to focus on the more profitable, and consequently more lurid, aspects of the collections, such as the freaks and oddities.

The economic prosperity of the latter half of the nineteenth century in America brought the rise of the robber barons, the merchant princes as they were called, who turned from procuring mines, railroads and banks to the amassment of books, great paintings, tapestries and European furniture. Men such as Andrew Carnegie, Andrew Mellon, J. P. Morgan, Henry Clay Frick, John D. Rockefeller and Henry Walters were known to be as ruthless in their collecting habits as they were in business. Often accused of having little taste, they were seen to accumulate masterpieces not for aesthetic reasons but as a source of immense power. The great banker J. P. Morgan bought whole collections intact; provenance being paramount, he acquired Catherine the Great's snuff box, Leonardo da Vinci's notebooks and Napoleon's watch. In the end Morgan donated almost half of his enormous collections to the Metropolitan Museum of Art in New York.

Europe, too, had its share of 'princes of finance', like the Hungarian nobleman Baron Heinrich Thyssen-Bornemisza, who seriously collected Old Master works with the fortune he inherited from the Thyssen magnates

The style of display traditionally considered appropriate for a gallery involved hanging paintings from floor to ceiling and interspersing them with sculpture and furniture, as shown in The Archduke Leopold's Brussels Picture Gallery, 1651, *by David Teniers the Younger (above) and* Ideal View of The Picture Gallery *(below) at Attingham Park, Shropshire (1769–1832).*

of Ruhrland steel. He housed his great collection of furniture, carpets, medieval gold objects and sculpture in a gallery he built at the Villa Favorita near Lugano, Switzerland, in 1932. Sir William Burrell, the late nineteenth-century Glaswegian shipping magnate and passionate collector, also accrued from three continents a vast collection of objects, including fine paintings, sculpture, ceramics, stained glass and metalwork spanning almost all periods of history. His collection is an example of a latter-day cabinet of curiosities, assembled with the same voracious spirit that had possessed the great collectors in the centuries before.

Dunrobin Castle in Scotland remains a place of grand Victorian fantasy. This lavish collection of big game trophies and stuffed creatures was amassed in the early part of the twentieth century.

The early years of this century saw the continued rise of the Rothschilds, the German merchant banking family who collected on a scale that dwarfs the efforts of most others of this period. All branches of the family collected, acquiring hoards of gold and silver objects, ivory, glass and rare books. Part of the collection is on view at Waddesdon Manor, Buckinghamshire, which was built by Baron Ferdinand de Rothschild, and, like the collections of kings, princes and robber barons, shows collecting as the prerogative of the rich.

Ironically, the nineteenth century, which saw such an increase in private wealth, also became known as the Museum Age, when institutional collecting flourished and the greatest number of important public museums were founded. Excessive wealth and nationalistic tendencies provided the backdrop for an interest in cultural heritage. Museums were formed around a core of private collections which were either bequeathed or purchased, with funding for buildings coming from both private and public sources. Museums founded at this time include the Museum of Fine Arts, Boston, Massachusetts (1870); the Metropolitan Museum of Art, New York (1872); South Kensington Museum in London (now the Victoria and Albert Museum, 1852); the Bavarian National Museum, Munich (1855); the Hermitage Museum in St Petersburg (1852) and many others.

After the deposition of the military dictatorship and with the emergence of Japan as a modern industrial state, the Meiji Restoration (1868) highlighted cultural awareness by opening in Tokyo both the Imperial Museum and the museum of the Ministry of Education. In China, however, things were different. Plagued by internal dissent and by the presence of British and French troops who occupied Beijing in 1860, much of its cultural heritage was dismantled. Many of the priceless imperial treasures found their way to London and Paris. It was not until the early twentieth century that the preservation of the national heritage was acknowledged as important with the founding of public museums, like the Palace Museum in the Forbidden City (1925) and the History Museum in Wu Gate of the Forbidden City (1926).

In our technological age, it is hard to envisage what could possibly inspire the same sense of mystery and even fantasy as the early cabinet of curiosities. Collecting in this century has become the preserve of the specialist, with taste and fashion changing at a rapid pace. At the

same time however, the definition of what is considered collectable is expanding daily and still includes much that is outside the domain of fine art. Yet, it is in the work of artists as disparate as Picasso and Damien Hirst – from Picasso's use of *objets trouvés* to Hirst's animals suspended in formaldehyde – that one can see a direct link to the Renaissance *Wunderkammer*'s aim to challenge and astonish the viewer. Surely, however, a truly modern cabinet of curiosity would be filled with the artefacts of space travel, pictures of recently discovered stars, examples of new surgical techniques, newly developed fabrics, lasers and the weapons of the modern age, all of which symbolize the quest for knowledge and look towards the future.

Above: Nature's overt oddities, like this double-tailed lizard, are preserved in John Hunter's eighteenth-century collection of specimens which illustrates the urge to contain and classify that fuelled evolutionary theories on adaptation of structure to function.

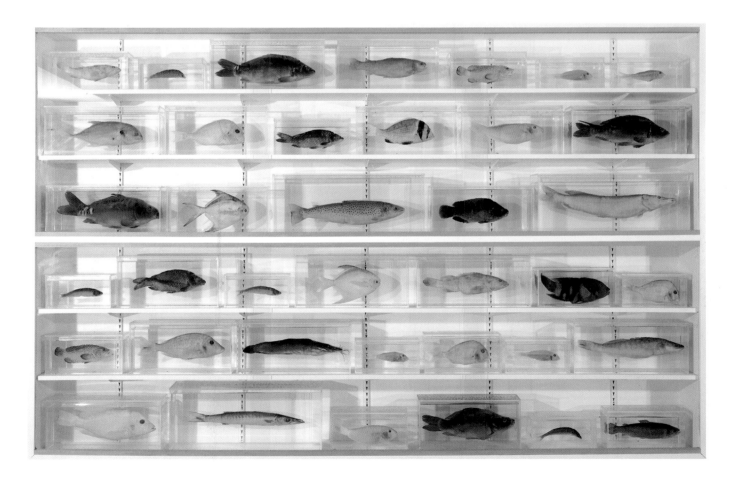

The art of shocking the sensibilities by suspending fish or sheep in formaldehyde contrived by the English contemporary artist, Damien Hirst, is hardly novel. His creations might be described as modern versions of the exotic taxonomic preparations made by enterprising natural history collectors of the seventeenth and eighteenth centuries, and exhibited in Wunderkammers *to stun, delight the eye and challenge the mind.*

The Psychology of Collecting

WHO KNOWS FOR CERTAIN what really motivates collectors. During the time when the cabinet of curiosities was the sign of an educated and enquiring mind, the purpose of accumulating unusual or distinctive objects seemed clear. In 1708 the pre-eminent German philosopher Gottfried Wilhelm Leibniz advised Peter the Great that *Wunderkammers* should 'serve not only as objects of general curiosity, but also as a means to the perfection of the arts and sciences'. In the same period, the Church saw its collection of precious objects as a way to glorify God. Collecting, however, has now become more widespread and specialized – nearly one in every three adults in North America and Europe collects something. Yet, surprisingly little is known about why and how people acquire certain kinds of objects.

Collecting is influenced not only by education and culture, but also by more complicated psychological issues, such as a compulsion to consume, a need to focus one's emotions, a quest for self-completion and a desire for control. Some argue that collecting is just another instinct found in the human psyche which affects some of us in the same way that the instinct to trade, cultivate, or manufacture affects others. Collecting has been defined as 'the process of actively, selectively and passionately acquiring, possessing and disposing of valued things, often removed from ordinary use and perceived as part of a set'. These objects may be found, bought, borrowed, made, traded or even received as gifts. Generally, it is agreed that collecting is a special type of consumption that differs from ordinary consumption as a motive for acquisition.

Collectors acquire not out of need but to enhance or expand their collection. Compared to the purchase of everyday objects, which are easily disposed of when obsolete, collecting implies passion and feeling for the objects themselves. This relationship is different from, though closely related to, the activities of accumulating and investing. Accumulators gather together unrelated objects which might seem like just a heap of junk to an outsider, but which are, to the person collecting them, a record of their life, and therefore meaningful.

Opposite: *Since the eighteenth century the trend towards specialization in collecting has usefully narrowed the competition and increased the chance of accumulating a collection that is truly unique. Having amassed over 500 examples of automatic robots, flying saucers and satellites, the owner of this collection has now moved on and has begun to collect smaller 1920s robots.*

In contrast, investors who collect often have little feeling about the objects being bought, as their interest lies more in the market value. While some may justify their habit of collecting by claiming that they are also investing, their primary motivation is probably part of the complex human phenomenon that makes it extremely difficult to define neatly a compulsion that has seized man for centuries.

Many adult collectors say that they inherited their taste for collecting from their parents. Robert Opie, an English collector of advertising and packaging materials, has little doubt that his parents' fondness for collecting children's books, toys and games rubbed off on him. He claims to have started collecting at the age of two, when he pulled a fossilized sea-urchin from the garden path, and it became the basis of a collection of stones and related items. As a young child, he went on to collect stamps, coins and the Lesney Matchbox series (his father encouraged him to write the price and date of acquisition on each box). This was what he calls 'my apprenticeship in collecting'. As he bought each object he also gathered information about the company that made it, the way they advertised their goods and knowledge about packaging in general.

Robert Opie founded the Museum of Advertising and Packaging in Gloucester after his terraced house overflowed with his obsessive collections of boxes, tins, bottles, trade signs and books that record the history of packaging and advertising. Born into a family of collectors, he was blessed with an upbringing that not only tolerated a magpie's mentality, but also taught him the 'art' of looking at things.

Covering this room with maps of the countries where her father worked has transformed these rather ordinary commodities into extraordinary, even sacred, items for this collector. Enshrining them in a private space further enhances their significance. This transformation from the ordinary into the revered by sentimental attachment to one's ancestors is a common phenomenon.

The brother of the author Alistair McAlpine claims that trains are in his blood: his grandfather built railways in the 1880s. His obsession has resulted in a railway line at his house, a complete working station, signal box and associated memorabilia – the collector himself can sometimes be found in full ticket collector's dress. These items have aesthetic appeal, but are also a vehicle by which the collector expresses himself.

Whether or not their parents collect anything is immaterial, however, as children are some of the most avid collectors, and their reasons for collecting seem to emphasize the fundamental appeal of some objects. There is no doubt that a child can get as much pleasure from discovering a rare comic book as an adult derives from owning a Van Gogh. Indeed, that child might well grow up to collect comic books rather than fine art. Although children do not always continue to collect, so many of them respond to that impulse directly that their habits can suggest more complicated trends. In a survey conducted in America at the turn of the century, every child between the age of eight and eleven was amassing between three or four collections at a time. Boys tended to collect stamps, birds' eggs, marbles

and rocks, while girls collected seashells, buttons, dolls and pieces of cloth. In the late 1960s a study in England recorded that even at the age of four, 80 per cent of boys and 66 per cent of girls collected something. According to recent statistics in the United States, children between nine and ten still maintain about three collections each, but with one big difference: they no longer collect so many found objects; today a much greater number are bought.

Children also demonstrate how collecting differs according to gender. Until recently the collecting of comic books was a boys' own zone, with many of the muscular heroes, like Batman and Spiderman, appealing largely to males. Even the comic-strip character Bart Simpson spends his own pocket money on comic books. Some

One former army air-traffic controller does not just collect models as toys; for him they represent the past and are his way of making it come alive. His collection of over a million model aeroplanes includes the Fokker plane flown by Baron von Richthofen during World War , the Spirit of Saint Louis, *in which Charles Lindbergh made his historic flight, and the very same planes he formerly scanned on radar.*

of the very early examples of comics seem to be suited to both sexes, whereas more recent titles are gender-specific, with publications on ponies and pop music aimed at girls. Despite this trend, most comic fairs are predominantly filled with male clients, suggesting that the comic collectors who started to amass their vintage *Dandy* and *Beano* when they were just learning to read, and who have continued to collect well into adulthood, are usually men.

History points to the predominance of male collectors assembling and researching their *Wunderkammers*. There were of course exceptions, including Queen Christina of Sweden and Catherine the Great of Russia, who, unlike their male predecessors, eschewed advice to pursue the 'perfection of the arts and sciences' and collected whatever

seemed to take their fancy. Surveys made during the latter part of this century contradict earlier findings, revealing that the number of women collectors has never been lower than men. Despite the greater fame of the male robber barons and their descendants, collectors of contemporary art are equally divided between both sexes, with Gertrude Stein and Peggy Guggenheim, two of the more prescient, pioneering collectors of the avant-garde. The seeming preponderance of male collectors may have had more to do with their style of collecting and penchant for flamboyant display than with the actual numbers of collectors.

One possible explanation for the misconception that collecting is a male-dominated activity is that often women's collections have been considered part of domestic history,

Above and opposite: *Freud's desk was covered with a collection of mainly phallic-shaped antiquities. Even his chair was part and parcel of his psychoanalytic interests. Freud started amassing objects just after the death of his father, finding in them a source of comfort.*

rather than a pleasurable or scholarly pursuit. New research is revealing that in the nineteenth century there were many important female collectors of porcelain and natural history materials, though they have been less well documented than their male counterparts. This may have to do with the fact that accumulations of blue-and-white china, lace bobbins, dresses, shoes and hats are not seen as collecting, but merely as an extension of everyday living. Even collections of dolls or jewellery are often viewed as motherly keepsakes to be passed on to daughters or grand-daughters rather than as collections valued in their own right. Men, on the other hand, acquire in a way which is deemed more serious, and their approach often suggests the traditionally masculine qualities of competition and aggression. This partly explains why male collectors tend to display and show their collections, while female collectors hide or use theirs.

Historically, their larger economic resources have also allowed men to acquire greater quantities and to focus on objects that are more specialized or costly and therefore more noteworthy or revered. Men tend to collect guns, fire-fighting equipment, armour, cars, trains and train memorabilia, all items that symbolize power and are immersed in sexual innuendo. Sigmund Freud was a keen collector of sculptural objects. His collection of over 4,000 Roman, Greek and Egyptian antiquities, displayed in his offices in Vienna and later at his house in Hampstead, England, are mostly phallic in nature and related, no doubt, to his theories on sexual symbolism.

Not surprisingly, men also collect more sports memorabilia and items like beer cans and beer mats, because of their interest in what these items represent; a practice that is the complete antithesis of the Renaissance male scholar, arranging his coins, busts and exotic artefacts, engrossed in the search for meaning. The scientist, with collections of instruments or natural history specimens, systematically catalogued, preserved and stored, is another stereotypically male collector. And though contradictions abound, there are established patterns of collecting dictated by gender.

Surveys point to another fundamental motive behind collecting – the desire for control. Underlying this feeling is the idea of possession. For many collectors their possessions allow them to manipulate their environment to form a special, private world of their own design. Many see the

For the shoe fetishist, the exact arch of the instep, curve of the heel and colour of the leather all contain an erotic charge.
Here, a pair of cleverly distorted shoes stands erect amongst a huddle of cylindrical oriental pots teeming with serviceable paintbrushes.
The tools of the artist's trade are captured by his camera with the inspiration of a painting.

items they collect as part of their extended self and so the desire for control can reflect larger emotional issues. It is somewhat ironic, though, to equate collections with control when there is always one item that is just right for the collection but out of reach, either because it is beyond the collector's pocket, or because it belongs to someone who will not sell. Nevertheless, the pursuit of the object is often what inspires the collector, drawing on the patience, prowess and competitiveness that we associate with the excitement of the hunt or quest.

Control is also linked with the need for symmetry and completeness in a collection. When a stamp collector was asked why he was taken with this kind of collecting he replied, 'because you know exactly what you are missing'. Many collectors enjoy filling a space, be it in their stamp album or in their collector's cabinet. Creating a visually appealing pattern in their display – though this seems to be of more importance in the West than in the Far East – is also a common motive. While the collector of sets is

often caught up in the pursuit of a single missing piece, no single item in a set is seen to be more beautiful or even more desirable than any other. In the end, it is the completed set as an entity in its own right that is the thing of wonder, not necessarily the rarity of one or more of the objects. It is the vision of the completed collection that drives the collector ever onwards. If one believes in the idea of collections as an extension of self, then it is the collector that is being completed not the collection.

We usually refer to individual collectors because collecting is almost always an individual pursuit. Of course, there are exceptions, like Victor and Sally Ganz, whose collection of works by Picasso and contemporary American painters was sold by their children towards the end of 1997 at Christie's in New York, many of the lots reaching record prices. The Ganzs' desire to seek out and learn about art was an obsessive passion they shared, and the constant wish to upgrade their collection continued for almost 50 years. Like many individual

Many collectors are motivated by the compulsion to preserve items or a particular moment in time for other people to enjoy in the future. Here, paper depictions of 'moonies', or sea trout, caught by fishermen in the lochs near this fishing lodge have been immortalized and recorded for posterity – each one a reminder of a successful catch.

collectors, they pursued the best, competing only against self-imposed standards of excellence. One Saturday in 1968 highlights their commitment. They set out to visit eight galleries, but Sally Ganz's feet gave after the sixth, when her husband continued the search. Like a compulsive gambler, this type of collector is thrilled by the action, the length and difficulty of the hunt, as well as the moment of triumph.

While many collectors are impressed by provenance – where an object came from and who made it – others, like the Ganzs, simply rely on their 'eye' in making their choice of what to acquire. This is perhaps most closely akin to the gambler's gut feeling. Some objects, in their shape or colour, are just aesthetically satisfying. In other cases, collectors rely on instinct, in the belief that the objects might prove more valuable over time. The collector is convinced that time and the market will one day justify what today seems like an obsession with a folly. Alternatively, collecting on instinct could be described

as a mere self-indulgence, though it has frequently resulted in the preservation of many of the world's masterpieces and therefore proved invaluable to the public at large.

The idea that some objects will increase in value is often used by people as a means of justifying their acquisitions. They like to believe that their collecting is, in fact, a form of investment. Limited editions of everything from baseball cards and watches to lithographs by well-known artists have helped to fuel the market and tempt potential collectors. These 'instant collectables' are usually manufactured at a small fraction of their retail prices and within days, sometimes even minutes, collectors eager to own the latest edition have pushed prices sky-high. Plastic telephone cards are currently the fastest-growing collectables, with four million collectors spanning the globe: in Japan they outnumber stamp collectors; in Germany there are over a million on record; and the French and British are not far behind. It appears that there is no card in existence that will not go up in value. Many of the cards

The first way we experience the world and form notions about normality and freakishness is through our bodies. Cultural influences might alter these ideas, but for the most part the bizarre holds its ground when shown next to the norm. On first inspection this grouping of hands – some human models, others not – is beautiful. However, several eerily realistic copies of the human hand are included, which elicit a macabre emotional response.

are privately published by clubs, charities and large companies who either want to add to their coffers or use the cards for advertising.

The rate at which these limited edition articles increase in value can be astonishing and could inspire the gambler's instinct in just about anyone. For example, in 1992 the Messerschmitt Owners' Club privately published 500 five-unit British Telecom phone cards which were quickly bought up by club members and collectors for £11 each, but within three years were worth £150. Yet even this gain pales in comparison to the standard issue 1983 Taiwanese card that was bought in 1995 by a Japanese collector for £28,000. This phenomenon, however, is not unique to telephone cards. Similar stories emerge in the market for Swatch watches, limited edition compact discs and Mercedes-Benz cars, all of which change hands at prices that are vastly higher than the retail price, often minutes after they leave the shops. There is no doubt that manufacturers have seen that gambling and collecting impulses, which are closely linked, can be easily exploited. Neither is there any doubt that collectors of Swatch watches, telephone cards and CDs are all acutely aware of how the market moves in their areas of collecting.

The complexity and mystery that lies behind the motives for collecting is matched by the diversity and quirkiness of the items people collect. From lavatory paper and air sickness bags to fine paintings and sculpture, there is no object too tawdry or too magnificent to be neglected by collectors. Prison inmates have been known to collect pubic hair; there are several such collections in New Scotland Yard's Crime Museum. In Holland during the early seventeeth century, the Dutch were so entranced by tulips imported from Turkey and Persia that 'tulip mania' seized collectors, enticing them to pay as much as 13,000 guilders, or the equivalent price of a grand Amsterdam town house, for rare bulbs.

It appears that collections not only project an image of the collector but illustrate how they see the world. For some, the objects have the ability to carry the past physically into the present; for others, they are symbolic of one's occupation, family heritage or appearance and are, therefore, autobiographical. In contrast, some people collect objects that are strangely appealing in a spiritual or sexual way.

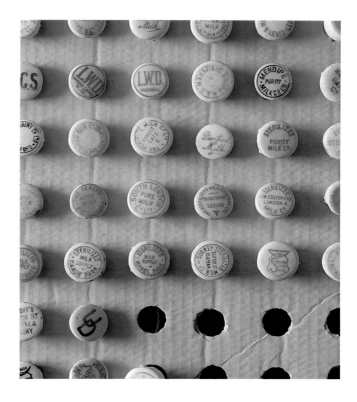

Collectors of milk-related objects, like these bottle tops, advise searching river banks, rubbish tips or even doorsteps for missing items. The compulsion to complete a collection is linked to a need for perfection.

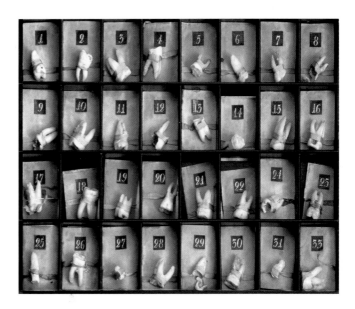

These teeth were all extracted by Peter the Great of Russia who fancied himself as a dentist. Could the passion to possess have been more fervent?

The word 'fetish' can be traced to the Portuguese *feiticos*, meaning 'charm', which described the holy medals and relics of the Christians in the fifteenth century, and later came to mean something 'magically active', like a totem or talisman. The term has lately been taken over by sexologists to describe objects collected and sometimes worn to satisfy a sexual goal or obsession. Women rarely display this instinct in comparison to men, who often relate their obsessive longing for an object to sexual desire. Geoff Nicholson, the author of the novel *Footsucker*, spent a year studying fetishists and discovered that such collectors were quite specific. 'It's got to be the right shape of toe, colour of nail varnish, kind of feet. That's what true fetishism is, it's about repetition. The fetishist is only interested in one thing – the same sexual release.' Shoes have always had strong sexual connotations, but if a women decided to purchase Rita Hayworth's gold leather evening shoes – worn during her scandalous romance with

Below: *Filled with an exotic mixture of architectural models, antique stone heads, bits of columns, framed pictures and clay urns, this room is a collector's nirvana. The items that have appealed to this collector are not simply an accumulation or hoard, but diverse sets of objects that have been amassed with a subjective slant.*

Opposite: *Myriad memories, both beautiful and a little disturbing, hang on every wall of this home and fill every shelf; certainly, this space belongs to no ordinary collector. Objets trouvés, be they tin bowls, plates, or farm implements, picked up on journeys through woods, beaches and scrap-yards, have been treated by collectors with the same – if not more – reverence than purchased items.*

Prince Aly Khan – would she be described as a fetishist, as a man certainly would be, or simply a collector? And would their motives be all that different?

Although most collectors are not considered socially abnormal, collecting is by no means an ordinary consumer activity. It is extraordinary in the passion and commitment people often feel. If the Smithsonian Institution in Washington, D.C., is considered the pinnacle of socially acceptable collecting, with stores containing 82,615 specimens of fleas, 12,000 Arctic fishing tools, 2,300 spark plugs and 14,300 sea sponges, then certainly we can legitimize

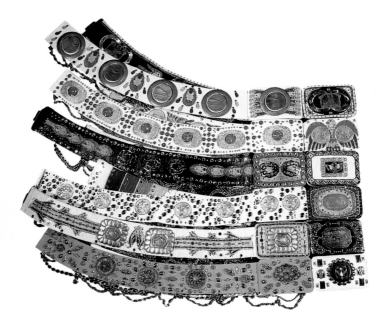

Above: *For the collector of Elvis's belts, there is, without doubt, an element of self-identification with the admired star. In the privacy of their bedrooms collectors of memorabilia frequently dress up in these items, be they clothing or accessories, to create a mise-en-scène – often complete with dim lighting, music and period surroundings.*

Opposite: *The Russian Princess Catherine Dashkov jokingly referred to her own collector's zeal as a 'kind of gluttony', a 'sickness, infectious like jaundice'. These words could also describe Scott Chinery's compulsive obsession for American guitars, which drove him to commission this unique set of contemporary blue archtop guitars to add to his existing accumulation of 1,000 vintage ones – making it the world's largest private collection.*

most personal collections no matter how ridiculous or eccentric they appear to be. Most research concludes that, while amassing collections can be a harmful addiction, for the vast majority, it is a relatively healthy activity, satisfying various needs at different times. Moreover, personal collecting, unlike that of most museums, does not generally suffer from elitism, racism and sexism.

One of the most popular collecting fields currently is memorabilia: associated items that belonged to or were produced by a particular person, place or period. These range from a phial of sweat from the late Elvis Presley (distilled from the sawdust that covered the stage where he performed) to guitars played by the late Jimmy Hendrix. Ian Fleming's typewriter, Lawrence of Arabia's dagger and Marlene Dietrich's Balenciaga evening coat have all fetched considerable sums at auction from people wishing to be associated with these celebrities. In the folklore of many cultures, owning something that belonged to somebody else is believed to bestow upon you the attributes of that person. To wear a piece of somebody else's clothing conveys even more power. Even in our civilized society, we see not just a second-hand typewriter but Ian Fleming's typewriter, not an old dagger but Lawrence of Arabia's dagger. In the collector's mind, these objects represent and assimilate the talents and the power of the former owner.

It is not only individuals who form an association through objects. A number of museums exhibit the brushes, paints and palettes of famous painters. Likewise, libraries own the pens, pencils and typewriters of celebrated writers. Some argue that there is little or nothing to be learned from these objects, that they only demonstrate a relationship between artist and museum. The public, however, are much taken with displays of this kind. For many people they are a way to identify with greatness.

The enthusiasm for memorabilia and ephemera, the minor transient documents of everyday life, is one of the most optimistic signs today in the world of collecting. This boom shows that collectors and the public are nowadays more interested in human beings than fine art. They want to know how those people dressed and how they lived. It appears that the information that memorabilia and ephemera can reveal is far more important to people today than the object itself.

This collecting of personal objects is relatively new. In centuries gone by people did not dispose of their goods and chattels in a way that made them available to collectors. Bankruptcy or financial pressure were the only real reasons for selling possessions. Homes only occasionally changed style, collectors rarely changed homes. Today collections come and go with great regularity in auction houses all over the world. Seldom is an entire collection sold as an entity. The value of its parts is nearly always greater than the sum of the whole. As in other areas of life in the twentieth century, money is what drives the auction houses and their clients. Collectors themselves move house regularly, or choose to live in a different country. Heirs often feel no real obligation to take on the responsibility of a family collection. As one historian of collectables puts it, 'material things are increasingly looked upon as disposable rather than the bondage gear of a lifetime'. Today, the excitement of the hunt and pride of possession vie with the liberation and financial gain of their disposal.

Still, like the *Wunderkammer*, which was created to project a particular personality or position in society, collections these days are arranged and presented within the

*This compulsive collector, fascinated since childhood with gas stoves, fitted an authentic 1930s New World cooker in his kitchen.
His collection now totals more than 100 examples which are crammed into every room in the house, making it almost impossible to get through
the front door. Collectors of what some might deem the prosaic see themselves as saviours who have rescued these objects from certain oblivion.*

home to convey not only the sophistication or importance of the pieces themselves, but also of the collector. Photographs of collectors' homes and offices are frequently published in books and magazines where they can be seen by anyone who is interested. The most involved collectors handle their collections, live with and even use or wear them, allowing their lives to become entwined with the pieces they have chosen so carefully. Some may keep fragile collections in cabinets or albums, or hide them like a magpie, but most often the objects that they collect are intended to be displayed. Their role is to be seen, so that they stamp the personality of the owner upon a space.

Not everyone knows quite how to create a successful living space around their collection, or how to create a collection to support their aims and ambition. In these cases an interior decorator might be called upon to design displays with the collector's personality in mind, or an 'expert in collecting' might be asked to create a collection and an image specifically for them. In Japan, collectors of Japanese pottery can purchase pieces by artists whose works have been awarded the status of Living National Treasures by the government. Highly prestigious, this official stamp of approval is used by some collectors to select items, often with no regard for the work's aesthetic

Studies have linked aesthetic preferences in collecting to extroversion and introversion. Extroverts are more likely to find themselves attracted to bold, vivid, realistic items while introverts tend to gravitate towards the romantic, subdued or refined. Although this aspect of collecting is not completely understood, links to temperament certainly seem to play a part. Might we conclude that this collection was amassed by an extrovert?

quality. Mihoko Koyama, one of the richest female collectors in Japan, chose to rely on a host of experts to assist her in the acquisition of over 1,000 objects of ancient Eastern antiquities, which are now housed in the Miho Museum in Shiga, Japan. There are some, however, who will simply go to one of the auction houses to purchase a collection that has been put together by a well-known collector or accumulated by several generations of a family because it comes complete with pedigree and status.

Regardless of what is collected or how the collection is gathered together, ranking high on most collectors' lists of activities must be the pure pleasure of arranging,

re-arranging and displaying their collections. Displays are made not only for pleasure, but also in order to get the best out of the items themselves, both aesthetically and intellectually. For collecting, in all its forms, is nothing if it is not visual. And like a stage set, the arrangement of a collection calls on the imagination to create an environment that highlights the inherent beauty and significance of the objects. In truth, however, there is nothing psychologically or morally wrong with hoarding or displaying your possessions, if you remember one fact: there is no object so wonderful or so rare that it is more important than the meanest human who would destroy it.

Styles of Display

NEITHER THE IMPULSE TO COLLECT nor the desire to display a personal collection are new, although the ways we carry these out in the twentieth century have changed dramatically. Evidence shows that early man collected objects for ritual and symbolic reasons, from the building of Stonehenge to the manufacture and exchange of highly polished jadeite and stone axes. The deliberate organization of hoards found in grave deposits proves that the practice of gathering objects for their aesthetic and spiritual associations and setting them out in a meaningful arrangement is age-old.

Like our ancestors of prehistory, we put great value on how our carefully selected objects are shown to the public. Where their stones were often placed in circles or piles of various shapes, we take equal care in arranging certain pieces next to, around, or away from each other. Though we may concentrate on each piece individually as we acquire them, often it is the relationship between them that is their most important aspect, whether it is their spatial relationship, their shape, history, or simply the significance they have for the collector. The layout of collected material in special, selected places may satisfy not only a collector's need to show off his or her treasures to friends, but also deeper intellectual, emotional and aesthetic needs.

The choice of what people acquire and how they display it is as deeply spiritual and highly personal as it was thousands of years ago. People still wear jewellery and collect objects that have a particular significance to them, because merely possessing the objects is not always enough. Many people get as much pleasure in exhibiting their collection as they do in tracking down the items themselves.

Just as there is no object too obscure to attract the attention of a collector, there is no single method of display that will satisfy the needs of every collection. Whether one has fallen under the spell of paintings or photographs, sculpture, textiles, ethnographic and folk art, natural specimens or household implements, collecting soon leads to arranging, finding the best place in the bedroom, kitchen or sitting-room to catalogue and celebrate the collection.

Opposite: *Catherine the Great of Russia was a 'china maniac'. She commissioned 40 allegorical figures of Saxe porcelain from the Meissen works to decorate her unique rococo follies at Oranienbaum, a palace built on the shores of the Gulf of Finland. The figurines, modelled by Kändler and Acier, are held on leafy stucco consoles; some are supported by monkeys and birds. As light pours through the spacious French windows, they shimmer and resonate in glorious splendour.*

The goal is to present the items in a unique manner that evokes in the viewer some of the sensation that the collector feels for them. There is also a certain status attached to a well-chosen, well-organized collection. That is why stamp collecting, which was in vogue for years, is today less fashionable in many societies where highly visible displays confer credibility on the collector.

Many, but certainly not all collections, are amassed within the framework of domestic life and so it makes sense to display them in the home. To class these things as 'room furnishings' is to overlook their primary function. However, they do play a role in creating a room or adding character to a space and are therefore intimately related to the interior design scheme.

People have been living with their collections for centuries. The ancient Greeks collected oriental carpets, wall hangings and ornate furniture from Persia to display in their homes; during the Renaissance, whole rooms were given over to 'cabinets of curiosities'; members of the English middle class of the eighteenth century filled their great halls with cartloads of artworks from Europe. Today, we continue to use our living space to display collected treasures.

The task of displaying your collection involves not only selecting a certain space within the house, but choosing or designing plinths, cabinets, shelves and containers, with the aim of producing a display where the objects can be properly appreciated. Pictures require considerable thought as to frames, mounts and methods of hanging, be it on picture rails, with hooks or with ribbon-covered wire.

Generally there is some underlying philosophy to the arrangement, without which the collection lacks spirit and therefore appeal. Just as the cabinets of curiosities were meant to further the developments of science, you might want to make a point about the rarity, vibrant colour or the oddness of the objects on display. The eccentric English collector Charles Paget Wade, who devoted his entire manor to displaying his massive collections, claimed: 'A room can be filled with innumerable things and yet have a perfect atmosphere of repose, if they are chosen with thought and care so as to form one harmonious background. The furniture should not stand out as a series of silhouettes, but merge into the background, the highlights being sufficient to show its form.'

Traditional methods of presentation – like the massed weapon displays seen in royal guard chambers and palaces, or the displays favoured by the great seventeenth-century collectors of oriental porcelain, provide a springboard for more contemporary displays, contributing a conventional framework within which new shapes, colours and materials can achieve an innovative effect.

What inspired the exponents of these masterful displays? While the two-dimensional geometric pattern displays in the guard chambers at Hampton Court may simply have been prompted by the shapes of the weapons, the starburst and circular arrangements of pistols, shields and sword blades may have been modelled on military decorations.

The massed arrangements of porcelain seen in many grand country houses led designers of the day to concoct ever more ingenious ways of accommodating these items. Shelves fitted in unexpected spaces and freestanding étagères, which allowed items to be arranged in diminishing tiers, were two such solutions. Their slender cylindrical forms may have been the stimulus for many of the pyramid-shaped displays, typical of the period.

You can learn a great deal from traditional arrangements such as these, incorporating the basic principles of traditional display whilst adapting them to the unique demands of a current collection. It is impossible to cover every variation of collection and display, but examples of some of the ways in which collectors of the past and present have approached the job of organizing and setting out their treasures have been included in the following pages as a source of interest and inspiration. Most collectors take real pleasure not only in amassing items to fit their collection but in organizing displays that exhibit the objects to best effect. This is where your own imagination comes into play, whether you are happiest with a group of portraits formally positioned along a wall or with an assortment of canoes suspended from the ceiling.

Egyptian pharaohs were buried with collections of furniture, stone objects, pottery and mummified cats; Chinese emperors were enclosed in their tombs with armies of terracotta warriors; the graves of Celtic chieftains were filled with gold; and Greek warriors had their armour nailed to a post by their tomb. Nowadays, however, most collectors prefer their possessions to see the light of day.

Like the Renaissance collectors, who wanted to create impressive displays that provided the visual thrill of finding the unexpected, collectors now want to show off the special significance of their particular collections. Whether these contain hugely valuable objects or mere household necessities, it is possible, using some flair and imagination, to share some of the joy of selecting those objects with each person who comes to admire them.

A collection of assorted colourful images dominates a wall from floor to ceiling, leading the eye up and down a plain staircase. The various colours and shapes of the ensemble give the room a vibrant rhythm, subtly tempered by the use of identical picture mouldings and the simplicity of the staircase. The collector's confidence in display is emphasized by the casual arrangement of quirky pieces on low tables and the choice of a brightly patterned carpet to complete the warm yet uncluttered effect.

Traditional Display

Historical arrangements that have stood the test of time can be regarded as 'traditional displays'. The great royal houses and palaces have long provided a backdrop for everything from arms and armour to porcelain, antiquities and paintings. These, along with the ways in which the renowned collectors of the past arranged their collections, have influenced our attitudes towards display, particularly those in domestic spaces. As the fields of collecting have changed, the demands of displaying collections have changed with them. What we view today as traditional has evolved with the changing patterns of trade and fashion.

Above: *Geometric displays of massed arms, hooked and stapled to a wall, create arresting shapes and eye-catching patterns. Despite the presence of largely eighteenth-century weapons, this arrangement at the King's Guard Chamber at Hampton Court Palace, reflects quite closely the original work of John Harris, the master of such displays.*

Right: *In the Great Hall at Chevening the patterns made using eighteenth-century tools of war echo those in the guard chambers at Hampton Court and St James's Palace. Although Harris had died before this display was executed, the two-dimensional rings of pistols and fans of bayonets were undoubtedly assembled with Harris' ingenuity in mind.*

Showing respect for the Swedish styles of the past and utilizing the straight upright shapes of halberds and swords, the 1920s residents of Kaflås Castle created an entrance hall of simplicity and elegance. The addition of an oil painting, depicting King Karl XII's prancing horse and a military parade drum, unifies the theme of the overall display.

There are various means by which we can deduce how and what was collected and displayed in the past. History can testify to trading patterns; catalogues of sales list the items in a collection and paintings of interior scenes and even portraits can reveal in fascinating detail precisely how objects in the background were arranged. Whether you want to recreate a particular period or merely use those examples as a source of inspiration, it is helpful to understand how and why certain traditional methods of display have come about.

As ambassadors from foreign lands paced the oak floorboards of the King's Guard Chamber at Hampton Court, around them on the walls were great cartouches of weapons. These displays of arms and military accoutrements were truly an impressive symbol of political power. In Britain the master of such arrangements was a certain John Harris of Eaton, who also devised elaborate weapon displays at Windsor Castle in Prince Rupert's guard chamber and later was responsible for their redisplay in the Queen's guard chambers. His ideas for creating patterns and compositions were highly original and had great influence at the time.

Harris went on to furnish displays for the guard chambers at St James's Palace and two rooms for the Prince of Denmark. These configurations used swords, pikes, muskets, pistols and armour set out in great cartwheels or large oval compositions; at the hubs were circular targets carved in lime with depictions of Medusa or lions' heads, many of which were supplied by the great master carver Grinling Gibbons, another influential designer. These displays seem to have been restricted to the whitewashed walls above the level of the wainscoting.

More informative displays, many arranged in chronological order in rooms dedicated to particular themes, were devised by Archduke Ferdinand II at Schloss Ambras, Innsbruck, in the late sixteenth century. One room contained the Archduke's own suits of armour, all exhibited on hidden wooden crosses and with painted flags hanging from the ceiling portraying mythical scenes. Another section housed suits of armour, formerly the possessions of kings and emperors, displayed in life-size cases, sometimes with a portrait of the former owner.

With the rising popularity of the neo-Gothic style in the nineteenth century, weaponry – particularly medieval arms and armour – came back into vogue. The country mansions of the new rich in Britain and America were incomplete unless they contained a display of military artefacts, most of which came from Continental Europe. Nowadays, attitudes towards weaponry are different, but these collections are still used as design elements or to illustrate a theme.

A collection of fine porcelain arranged on diminishing tiers of marble above a stately fireplace creates an impressive symmetry of pattern. Larger corresponding pieces on the hearth emphasize the turreted shape of the display and balance the overall effect of grandeur. The stacked arrangement of the paintings flanking the fireplace is typical of the late seventeenth century when the interior of this English country home was remodelled.

Arms and armour may have made up some of the earliest and most prominent displays of collected objects, but they soon began competing for space with numerous other artefacts. The seventeenth-century sale catalogue of perhaps the world's greatest private collection, that of King Charles I of England, included sculpture, paintings, prints and drawings, textiles, furniture, arms and armour, as well as horological, mathematical and musical instruments. That a tapestry in the sale fetched many times the price of a masterpiece by Titian attests to the changing attitudes of collectors. Interestingly, however, a painting of the king and queen reveals that this extensive collection was probably not on view as we might expect. The painting, executed in 1635 by Gerard Houckgeest, shows Charles I and Queen Henrietta Maria dining in public, but there is no evidence in the picture, apart from two paintings hung on the walls, of the treasures that the king possessed. Clearly the custom was to keep most of the collection hidden away.

The end of the seventeenth century heralded a mania for all things related to China. Objects such as lacquer-ware and porcelain vases, bowls and tea services were passionately collected and the methods of display favoured by the collectors became extremely influential. Prized for their colours and decorative qualities, export porcelain was the height of fashion in Europe for some 80 years.

In England, Queen Mary II led the way in amassing and displaying these pieces. Her taste, along with her collection of thousands of pieces of all descriptions, was formed in Holland where she lived until she came to England with her husband King William, in 1689. Her Kensington Palace inventory of 787 pieces provides us with information about porcelain arrangements of this period. Useful objects, such as cups, mustard pots and teapots were displayed together, while decorative objects, such as *blanc de chine* figures, were placed over the mantelpieces, in cabinets, or on shelves and pedestals. Dolls' houses of the period reflect a trend for arranging porcelain on shelves set into the wall and on individual brackets. In addition, each room at the palace had a variety of pieces in it, arranged according to colour and shape. 'In the Old Bedchamber', the inventory tells 'the over-mantel arrangement included seventy-four pieces

arranged on shelves forming a pyramid, with pieces of yellow, brown, purple and blue mixed together.' Arranging pieces on overmantels is a familiar practice today.

When the Queen died in 1694, King William transferred much of her collection to Arnold Joost van Keppel, who was made Earl of Albemarle in 1696. He transported it to Huis de Voorst in Holland where the King's architect,

In the Glass Cabinet at the Rosenborg Palace, Copenhagen, a wealth of Venetian glass adorns the walls and is reflected in mirror glass to spectacular effect. The collection of 1,000 pieces of glass was presented to King Frederik IV of Denmark by the City of Venice during his stay there in 1709. Installed in 1714, the cabinet was inspired by the oriental porcelain and mirror glass at Schloss Charlottenburg in Berlin.

Daniel Marot, may have assisted in creating rooms covered with carved wood panelling, with paintings hung over the mantels and doors and tapestries draped over tables and walls. The porcelain cellar overflowed with mounted Japanese and Saxon pieces. Before the contents were sold off in 1744, descriptions of the house record that porcelain was placed inside the fireplaces during the warmer months. Many Dutch cabinets of this period were constructed with cornices designed for the display of garnitures of porcelain and often fitted with glass fronts.

In eighteenth-century Holland, collections of porcelain continued to play a dominant role in the decoration of interiors. Popular arrangements included loading tea tables with heaps of coffee and teacups, teapots, saucers and sugar bowls that were, for the most part, decorative rather than functional. By the mid-eighteenth century, when porcelain had become commonplace, collectors became more discriminating. The enthusiasm for all things Chinese led to the production of new types of furniture, such as intricate wall sconces and elaborate looking-glasses, that

echoed the oriental style of the porcelain. Sometimes the collected objects themselves were used to form furnishings. In France, panels of lacquer work were incorporated into the designs of commodes, while Venetian designers and English furniture-makers of the period found inspiration in the colours and ornamental forms from China.

Looking like giant Chinese lacquer boxes, 'china-mania' buildings were built to house such collections. The interiors were often panelled with imitation lacquer, decorated with raised and gilded latticework, or covered with painted yellow silk or rose-coloured rice paper; all serving as a background for shelves teeming with eclectic mixtures of Chinese and Japanese porcelain figures, vases and urns.

By the end of the century this trend was waning, but some remarkable Chinese-inspired fantasies had been produced, including the Palazzina La Favorita outside Palermo, the whimsical Royal Pavilion, Brighton, built in 1816 for the Prince Regent, the rococo Chinese and Montagnes Russes follies at Oranienbaum, the Japanese Palace in Dresden built by Augustus the Strong, King of Poland, and the five-room oriental pavilion in the grounds of the Royal Palace of Drottningholm, Sweden.

As 'china-mania' interiors had been designed around and dedicated to porcelain, so in the eighteenth century, a craze developed for purpose-built sculpture rotundas – created to house the many collections being assembled at the time. One magnificent example is Robert Adam's design for William Weddell at Newby Hall, Yorkshire. This space, modelled in the style of a Roman interior, consists of two square rooms and a central rotunda, complete with apses and niches. Fine plasterwork adorns the ceiling and the backgrounds are decorated in polychrome with central circular panels filled with birds and playing cards. Many of the elaborate rectangular and cylindrical pedestals for the works were also designed by Adam, and the 12 George III wall brackets set just above head height originally supported oil lamps.

In other famous English houses, like Syon House and Kedleston, the entrance halls were crammed with sculpture and at Castle Howard, Sir John Vanbrugh provided corridors leading off the hallway especially for the display of sculpture; they became known as 'antique passages'. A drawing by Sir William Chambers of Charles Townley,

Opposite: *Row upon row of copper saucepans, suspended by their handles on wooden beams, fill an expansive kitchen wall, showing that groups of useful objects can be set out not only for ease of use but also to delight the eye. A mass display of items arranged in a systematic, melodious manner lifts the gloom of this utilitarian space.*

Above: *The Long Gallery at Powis Castle, Wales, is decorated with exquisite* trompe-l'oeil *panelling and ornate plasterwork, painted in repeating patterns with the Elizabethan family coats of arms, and completed in the late sixteenth century. Ancestral portraits, sculpture and porcelain arranged in the style of the late eighteenth century are also on display.*

The glass-fronted square, octagonal and bell-shaped display cases are an integral part of this 'room of birds' at Sheringham Hall, Norfolk. In the nineteenth century it became fashionable to mount stuffed birds in elaborately constructed cases with naturalistic settings, rather than simply placing them on plinths or stands. The cases could be moved from room to room or stacked one on top of another against the walls.

one of the great dealers and connoisseurs of the period, reveals an entrance hall with walls adorned from floor to ceiling with antique marble reliefs and sculptures.

The great dilettante collectors of the mid-eighteenth century, who made their way to Italy to acquire classical sculpture and paintings, devised new styles of display for their grand rooms of entertainment. Slabs of marble, alabaster and granite that might have been part of a frieze, were adapted to form the tops of tables or were placed over mantels and doors. A portrait by Daniel Mytens of Thomas Howard, 2nd Earl of Arundel in his seventeenth-century sculpture gallery – the first such gallery recorded in England – shows one such collection. Arundel sits pointing a baton, the symbol of his hereditary office, at two rows of life-size marbles mounted on purpose-made plinths.

The British passion for collecting objects from abroad increased in intensity during the nineteenth century. The wealth created by Britain's booming industry and her colonies allowed collectors to continue to plunder parts of Europe that had been torn apart by wars. The vast quantities of pieces collected led to even more cluttered displays during this period. Moreover, not only were there quantities of items available in conventional areas of collecting, but boatloads of exotic imports arrived from India, Egypt and the Middle East, along with natural and man-made curiosities from Australia and Polynesia.

Massed collections displayed wall-to-wall were popular during Victorian and Edwardian times. This was also the great age of taxidermy: mounted horns and heads of deer, moose and other hunted animals became fashionable

On the Edwardian library table in the centre of this library are eighteenth-century models of staircases and a bronze replica of the column from the Place Vendôme, commemorating Napoleon's victories. The group is balanced by the imposing stature of Napoleon on horseback that is silhouetted against the window. The refined character of the room is strengthened further by the polished wooden floor, the architectural mouldings, the pictures on the walls, and the sixth-century Greek helmets adorning the Regency shelves.

features in grand country houses as well as palaces and castles. The salon at Castle Konopischt in Bohemia boasts a typically opulent interior decked out in trophies interspersed with large oil paintings of the animals in the wild.

Today, the interest in collecting has broadened to include almost every kind of object. Although the market is strong in modern limited editions of items as diverse as fountain pens, phone cards and couture clothing, for many it is the vintage models that are fulfilling their obsessions. These items may not be the rarest nor the most expensive, but they are icons of their age, and, as one expert in the field of collecting has noted, 'They are the ultimate prizes for collectors, an attainable holy grail'. There is a definite trend for such items to be worn or shown ostentatiously for all to see rather than being hidden away.

At the other end of the scale, the digital revolution has allowed the Microsoft giant Bill Gates to fulfil the dream of a lifetime: on the walls of his home he displays video images of over 100,000 great paintings to which he owns the electronic rights, an example of traditional display that exploits technological advances to the full.

Looking at these examples from past and present, we can see how collecting and interior display have become linked, how whole rooms can be devoted to showing off a collection, either in a reconstruction of its original environment or in purely decorative arrangements. As Roman busts, weapons, Chinese porcelain and hunting trophies inspired new styles of display that we would now call traditional, collectors today can build on the fashions and designs of the past to create equally exuberant displays.

Innovative Display

Many of the world's great innovators have acknowledged the past as a source of inspiration. The fashion designer the late Gianni Versace claimed that many of his designs were modern interpretations of historical dress, nurtured by the appreciation of classical forms in ancient Greek sculptures and architecture that surrounded him as a child in Calabria. His pleated dresses, flatteringly wrapped and tied around a woman's body, resembled the tunics of Roman emperors. His bright patterned outfits contained elements reminiscent of Celtic designs. Technological advances in fabric manufacture, as well as in methods of production, enabled him to continue to innovate.

Above: *The lively gestures of these whimsical fairground figures come to life in a light-filled steel-and-glass display tower that zigzags its way through a five-storey villa in Antwerp.*

Opposite: *Creative twists abound in the house of fashion designer Liza Bruce and husband Nicholas Alvis Vega. With unusual objects in unexpected places, a Louis XV-style sofa upholstered in lead and wheelbarrows as plinths, here is inspiration for even the most adventurous collector, whether the scheme is contrived or accidental.*

By borrowing freely from the past, today's collectors can also adapt and modify display methods to ensure that they too find imaginative contemporary solutions.

It is never easy to be truly original in your thought or in how you approach a subject. To think of new areas of collecting and new ways of displaying those collections is a pretty tough assignment. For collectors, originality comes largely by drawing on history and adapting old ideas for new needs. In addition, the ease of modern travel has brought inspiration from all over the world, from landscape, design and art, to materials, the use of colour and primitive decorative markings. These influences produce one-of-a-kind methods of display that are often regarded as bizarre and difficult to accept, but the simple reason for this may be that we do not understand where the ideas come from.

When the Sydney Opera House was built, it was considered a highly unusual solution for such a purpose. To come to grips with it, the public tried to compare it to what they understood: could it be the white sails of ships in the harbour, or a budding flower? The building was, in fact, inspired by a nautilus shell. If a similar opera house was built, it would no longer be extraordinary. Fortunately, history points to a continuous flow of extraordinary solutions and so the bizarre flourishes, along with the feelings of shock and surprise they aim to provoke.

Sir John Soane must rank as one of the most imaginative architects of his age, if not of all time. He was also a prolific collector, and the solutions he arrived at for displaying his collections in his London home were certainly considered unconventional in the late eighteenth and early nineteenth centuries. He thought of his buildings as ancient ruins and even had his perspectivist-cum-assistant draw his home as it might appear in 2,000 years' time. His collections of architectural fragments, ancient sculptures, drawings and paintings form mass displays on every wall and shelf. Some rooms are painted a deep red, a colour based perhaps on fragments of wall plaster he brought back from his visit to Pompeii. He used a conjuror's eye when it came to the placement of mirrors, putting them behind exhibits and above books to create the illusion of expanded space and even the impression of another room.

Soane's use of light, too, was magical. Placing windows and skylights in unexpected places, he showed off his collections brilliantly. At night he carefully placed hundreds of candles to magnify the reflective effects. In his breakfast parlour he employed technically advanced methods, using concealed skylights fitted with yellow glass, for example, to create the illusion of sunlight, and placing more than 100 pieces of mirror glass all around to produce a kind of spatial sorcery. Walls fold back to reveal a space several stories high, reminiscent of the great classical spaces Soane admired on the Grand Tour.

His most ingenious achievement is his purpose-built gallery for displaying his collection of paintings and drawings. The walls are a series of hinged panels, hung with works on both sides, thus more then doubling the available wall space. Even the maze of rooms in the basement is filled with cast fragments, and one room contains a ruined abbey complete with tombs. Odd and humorous at the same time, the arrangement is one of pure genius.

His is the kind of magic one should strive for when conceiving an innovative display, the melding together of fantasy and humour. Like Soane, some collectors commission or design their ideal house to display their collections, disobeying all the classical or modern rules of restraint or beauty. The deconstructed house of fashion designer Liza Bruce and her husband Nicholas Alvis Vega fits this description. In their redesigned house, the pipes have been exposed to form odd geometric shapes within

the rooms. Lead is used both on a staircase, and as upholstery on the furniture. Wheelbarrows serve as tables and plinths for marble statuary; mirrors are hung at odd angles to catch unlikely reflections, and collections of objects are displayed in irreverent ways. Even the garden grows inside through holes in the walls, reminding one of the surrealism of *Alice in Wonderland*. While the house is filled with objects that look as if they come from a scrapyard, it suits the deconstructed nature of the scheme. The whole house is an adventure *par excellence* and a unique environment for a highly individual collection.

Bruce and Vega are among a number of people who have chosen to create a house around their collection. In the twentieth century, a rash of modern palaces for contemporary art continue to spring up, and none more outrageous than those on the west coast of America. Here, we have progressed beyond the cliché of displaying expensive sculpture in the foyer. Cement, corrugated metal, and glass bricks are used both inside and out, providing double-height spaces with natural ventilation and masses of light – ideal display areas. Celebrating the pleasures of light and space can be risky but the results can be outstanding. Rather than reproducing a structure that reflects the past in an unoriginal manner, many collectors have extended the principles of modernism to produce stunning interiors showing, for example, a collection of Abstract Expressionist or Pop Art alongside modern or antique Chinese furniture, or hanging pieces of classic cars from

Minimalist contemporary architecture and illusionistic spaces draw the eye into their depths with mesmerizing and sometimes disorientating results. Looking at Accelerazione *by Mario Merz leaves the viewer unsure of which way is up. Even using the surrounding artworks as bearings demands acute eye–brain performance.*

Using every inch of available space, this collection of fine china is a visual wonder, reminiscent of the extraordinary ceiling in a room at the Santos Palace in Lisbon. There, a specially constructed pyramidal ceiling is clad in blue-and-white late Ming plates, held in place by a wooden framework.

the ceiling above a large contemporary installation such as a circle of stones. The combination of objects itself does not matter as long as the result is startling.

Often it is the collection as well as the display that is innovatory. Lawn mowers, milking machines, petrol pumps, shop signs, surfboards and fairground figures – there are in this age no limits to what can be collected and displayed in a home. Advertising material that is made for display, from a life-size fibreglass superman to the plastic cones that adorn ice-cream parlours, is a fast-growing field. Although such ad hoc displays have the potential to become hybrid monsters, when they are executed well they are strange, thought-provoking, and possibly inspiring.

Recent advances in technology permit designers to produce spaces that allow traditional collections to be displayed in ever more challenging ways. Complicated metal-and-glass cabinets extending in a vertical zigzag make a highly imaginative display unit that can be used to house almost anything, though large items will inevitably produce the most dramatic result. There is no part of a house that cannot serve as a background for a collection: even in a stairwell you can find room for narrow cabinets.

Nor, for that matter, is there a part of a house that a collection cannot be found to fill. The centrepiece of the new British Library is a six-storey glass tower housing George III's private library, which surges up from the basement, serving as both a book stack and a display case, striking a fascinating balance between the familiar and the sublime.

An innovative display can impart humour, be playful and entertaining, offering extreme incongruities, or visual 'one-liners'. An eye-catching assemblage can be made by placing zany collections or single items in ordinary spaces. When displayed against a whitewashed wall, lavatory handles and chains cease to be utilitarian objects and are transformed into enchanting pieces in their own right. Pebbles, pine cones, broken glass, scrap metal,

An obvious, yet quirkily improvised solution to storing a country hat collection. Teetering on top of a classical marble bust, the hats poke fun at the serious expression upon the figure's face, creating a light-hearted mood in an imposing entrance hall.

Dispensing with conventionalism, the owner of this impressive drawing room has found unusual ways of showing off his startling collection of skis, paddles, snowshoes and tomahawks – all amassed during his official assignments overseas. Around the fireplace, in the space usually reserved for displays of impressive ancestral portraits, treasured mementoes have been hung on sheets of chicken wire – an unlikely material to find in such an illustrious setting.

An eerie shrine, possibly intended as an homage to the glories of life and the certainty of death, displays an eclectic mixture of natural and artificial curiosities; its discordant, but thought-provoking configuration produces a surrealist's ideal 'cabinet of curiosities'.

Above: *A collection of ex votos – small religious thank-offerings, crosses, diminutive metal charms in the shape of arms and legs, keys, stomachs and faces of ladies, and groups of coins – nothing very rare or valuable, tacked to the surface of an aged wooden door. The genius of this display is in the collector's ability to arrange such a disparate group of objects together, against an unlikely backdrop, and to do so with such out-standing success.*

Above right: *Arranged in towering heaps that echo the shapes of the minarets on the Blue Mosque, these stacks of Hermès boxes impart a refreshing modicum of humour to an otherwise austere environment. Like many disposable objects, when arranged en masse, their variation in size, shape and colour can be utilized to produce impressive arrangements of stunning simplicity.*

Right: *A motley selection of historical domestic paraphernalia, such as milk bottles, butter churns or thatchers' knives can, in the hands of an enthusiastic collector, be shown together to beautiful effect. Here, humble lavatory chains, both antique and modern, are hung at various lengths against whitewashed brick-work above a range of chamber pots to produce a minimalist's perfect display.*

In most homes, a Corsican mountain goat resting on a drawing-room sofa would appear out of place, but in this eccentric residence the stuffed animal looks perfectly at ease. For some collectors, there are no restrictions when it comes to arranging and displaying their exotic or unconventional wares among their more formal treasures, such as oil paintings and grand furniture.

coins, keys, all manner of found objects that traditionally have been placed in labelled drawers or cabinets, might instead be arrayed on a door or wall. Similarly, rather than being thrown away, disused maps and boxes can be used to paper or decorate a room. When the mundane is brought together with the unlikely, the two together can form a statement that startles and amuses.

The ceiling is uncharted territory when it comes to display. Yet, as history so elegantly points out, it can be exploited with dramatic and effective results. A space that might once have been painted with mythical scenes can be used to display unframed paintings, rows of plates, Ikat fabrics or Chinese robes. Almost any item that can be displayed on a wall can be displayed equally, if not more successfully, on a ceiling. You can even mimic the

historic star formations created on the walls of royal residences with weapons, adding an element of surprise by substituting long-handled garden tools.

These displays demonstrate real courage, the sort that only the dedicated innovator can demonstrate. They pass with ease the 'I've never seen anything quite like it in my life' test for innovation. You could even go so far as to say that, had these displays been described before they were carried out, they would have provoked serious doubts. But never lose heart when searching for truly original, unconventional or unlikely solutions. Whether you start with something traditional or decide to begin completely from scratch, it is letting your imagination run wild that makes it possible to forego the obvious in pursuit of the remarkable.

Pictures and Photographs

Above: *A busy collage of prints, postcards and family photographs takes pride of place above the fireplace in this informal sitting-room. The significance of this personal collection of mementoes for the owner is stressed by its position at the room's focal point.*

Opposite: *The joy of collecting is not limited to viewing an array of objects; it also comes from handling the treasures you own. Collectors of books, for example, find deep satisfaction in casually leafing through a favourite volume, while art collectors enjoy selecting a single picture from a stack of many others to admire its individual qualities. In this overflowing display, ceramics and art sit amicably alongside the books.*

Enthusiastic collectors of paintings, prints and photographs will inevitably end up with more than they have space to hang. This should not be a worry, however, as there are many ways of displaying pictures; they do not have to be hung on walls, as a visit to any painter's or photographer's studio will confirm.

One solution is not to hang them at all. Leaning pictures against the walls, or placing them on shelves, can be an intriguing way to present a large number of works and make them accessible for close scrutiny. A stack of pictures, even some facing a wall, will evoke interest. Placing individual works on a low-seated, straight-backed chair will allow you and friends to discuss their merits in comfort, as well as providing an alternative to hanging them on a wall. This method of display has the added bonus of inviting the viewer to examine the back, with its record of previous owners and exhibitions, which would not be possible if the picture were hung. Such informal presentation prompts a far greater intimacy than staring at a picture on a wall. Do not, however, limit your stashes to just the sitting-room: be daring and use the hall, kitchen and even the bathroom if space and ventilation allow.

The American painter Cy Twombly leans his paintings against the walls of his Italian coastal villa along with ornate empty picture frames and French and American flags. This rather casual approach creates a relaxed atmosphere. It also leaves you with additional wall space and endless opportunities for ever-changing compositions.

There are, however, disadvantages to exhibiting your collections in this manner, not least the problem of cleaning around them. Ultimately, hanging pictures is all about matching the size and mood of the work to the scale and mood of the room, but bear in mind that a room's colour and contents will have an effect on how large it appears. To hang a painting, print or photograph on a wall isolated from any other work of art may be the simplest display in principle but it is the hardest to make work in practice, as it will become a focal point in the room, thereby affecting the overall decorative scheme of the room. An isolated work must relate to the colour and shape of the room, the curtains and furniture. Positioning a sculpture nearby to diffuse the emphasis can ease the process of establishing a relationship between a single painting and a room.

The sculpture can then be repositioned until you find that the composition of the room, the painting and the sculpture create a 'rhythm of quality', a natural harmony. On a more practical note, it is much easier to move a sculpture around than to repaint an entire room or to re-hang a picture.

Alternatively, show pictures of all sizes by 'papering' almost every inch of wall space, as in eighteenth- or nineteenth-century illustrations of great private houses and art exhibitions. If you opt for this postage-stamp system of hanging, you will need to relate the compositions and colours of the works to each other rather than the room itself. This is best tried out on the floor beneath the wall you intend to use, where works can be reshuffled as necessary until you have achieved the right balance. Standing on a chair or ladder will give you a bird's-eye view of the layout and allow you to have a sense of its final composition. Only when the arrangement reaches an aesthetically pleasing whole should you begin to hang. Do not dismiss the option of re-framing to achieve the right effect; a frame that suits a painting in isolation can be a considerable disturbance to the harmony of an ensemble. Again, sculpture can help to achieve a balanced effect. Stand sculptures in front of or alongside a picture and never be afraid to take the plunge and hang three-dimensional objects, which were originally destined to be freestanding, as part of a composition.

Continuous lines of works hung for the specific purpose of study is a way of displaying paintings that was developed by the Italian historians of the late eighteenth century. Consumed by the development of painting, they

Leaning paintings against a wall or perching them on easels will allow a collector to re-arrange artworks at a whim. Such flexibility may be too haphazard for some, but the owners of this Parisian atelier enjoy mixing their collections of 1940s and 1950s items with contemporary furniture. Making regular alterations to your room can provide a stimulating environment.

Against a backdrop of books and alongside a skilfully placed sculpture, these paintings occupy every conceivable space, including a book easel usually occupied by an open volume. Pictures lend themselves especially well to being displayed on folio stands, lecterns and revolving bookstands.

Against citrus walls, distressed wooden troughs support assorted overlapping architectural and historical prints and photographs.
The narrow black-and-white frames complement those of giltwood, and the lime green and deep red striped silk brocade covering the French
'fainting couch' enriches the harmonious colour scheme.

collected works for their historical value rather than their artistic quality. This method has influenced the displays that can be seen in many European royal palaces and public galleries, including the Louvre, as well as private houses.

A single row of paintings hung on every wall can be monotonous, but it does suit some types of work and certain spaces. Vintage photographic prints, for example, identically mounted and in similar frames, create a startling minimalist interior when hung in a continuous line at eye level on a plain wall. It is helpful if the other furnishings in the room match this austerity.

For those entranced by huge gallery-like living spaces, large contemporary paintings set against a wall on their own, like a meditating Buddha, will recreate the feel of a contemporary art gallery. Yet, while such an atmosphere is suitable for certain works, it is not always appropriate; some paintings look best when surrounded by other works.

If an intimate studio-like space is more desirable, subtle architectural changes can help, or, adopting a less drastic approach, wall coverings, cushions, lamps

or flooring can be altered. In such settings, the size and presence of the work are of utmost importance. The vitality of a large triptych by Francis Bacon could hardly create a harmonious atmosphere in a small space. Instead, one might choose to display Japanese wood-block prints, known as *ukiyo-e* – 'pictures of a floating world' – with their softness of colour and calming scenes. A minimalist work can also help to evoke calm and tranquility, especially if it is hung in a small space.

Those who say that 'there is nothing worse than seeing one large picture alone' would probably add, 'except possibly a small one'. Small pictures can be problematic, despite the apparent flexibility their size bestows upon them. Many collectors find it convenient to sprinkle them between books or other ornaments on shelves. Small pictures can also be leaned against a wall when set on top of a shelf or mantelpiece. You may choose to hang smaller works within displays of objects, such as wall-mounted porcelain. They can be arranged in symmetrical formations, or grouped round a larger work, particularly

Left: *Frank Lloyd Wright furniture and a row of prints combine to create an atmosphere of serenity. The owner has played with the subtleties of lighting, colour and texture to set off the collection of prints to its best advantage. The look is calm and uncluttered – an effect that all but the keenest magpie collector might hope to achieve.*

Below: *Fragments of ceramies, bits of marble, antique pottery and Islamic tiles mingle with textiles and paintings in frames of different sizes and styles in this souk-like assortment of wonders. Unable to resist the urge to procure, the collector has given in to compulsion, buying objects on impulse and finding a home for them later. As a result, the room resonates with passion and the temptation to touch its rich textures.*

Opposite: *In an artist's home a nest of Renaissance frames is displayed as a work of art. Carved in giltwood or painted with scrolling ornamentation, objets d'art such as these were once underrated but are now used as objects to be displayed in their own right.*

one of artistic or dynamic significance. A visit to a grand country house can be worthwhile just to see how the latter method has been used to great effect in the past.

Serious collectors in possession of a large number of images might consider reviving the seventeenth-century tradition of using a small room for the display of small-scale paintings, turning the space into a 'jewel' cabinet. Those with only a modest budget can recreate a traditional eighteenth-century print room by covering the walls from floor to ceiling in closely spaced, unframed prints. Prints traditionally mounted in gold or black frames can appear in non-traditional places, such as bathrooms or cloakrooms.

Those who like the option of changing their displays frequently might want to make use of artists' easels to allow them the freedom to replace one picture with another whenever the impulse strikes. This method works well for both framed and unframed pictures. Those who truly find static displays a bore can set works into moveable frames on wheels, so that with just a gentle nudge an entire arrangement will be transformed. On doors, above doorways, over a bed, against screens, or even screwed onto ceilings to mimic the painted grandeur of historic palaces – there is nowhere a picture cannot be hung effectively. The only rules are your own.

Sculpture

Whether you are attempting to display the noble head of a Roman, a gilt bronze statue of a Nepalese *bodhisattva*, or a reclining marble figure by the contemporary sculptor Henry Moore, the final effect – dramatic or low-key – should feel unforced and harmonious.

Many collectors of sculpture do not remain faithful to a particular period. Their homes are an accumulation of all types of objects from different epochs. This time-honoured aesthetic usually calls for an abundance of sculpture, with

Antique busts glance sideways and downwards from an illuminated shelf set high above an artist's entrance hall, creating an atmosphere of humour and surprise. The artist has found an ingenious method for hanging artworks, using a length of thin wire that runs below the shelf. A paint palette and paintbrush have been secured on the wall, while two artist's maquettes observe the scene from their perch on a nearby shelf.

barely a surface left uncovered. Sensitive to complementary forms and colours, carved wood sculptures might be found alongside twentieth-century bentwood furniture, or Greek white marble figures in a room where both floors and tables are covered in richly coloured oriental carpets.

Like the Victorians before them, many people prefer cluttered interiors with items arranged in a seemingly random fashion throughout the room or house, yet even the most random of displays will need some kind of structure.

When a composition is made up of a few very strong pieces, with the spaces in between filled with intriguing, if less visually stimulating, objects, such interiors can work very well. A room that demonstrates such an attitude towards display suggests a treasure house – luxurious, lavish and full of interest. Each piece will tell its own story, reacting and playing off other sculptures, creating a continuous dialogue, and resulting in a room that is overflowing with visual pleasure.

The austerity of this chrome and white kitchen is broken up by three drawing models, striking different poses, each in front
of a separate panel of the large window. The striking arrangement evokes the grandeur of aristocratic homes of the eighteenth century,
where great halls were purpose-built for the display of ancient marble sculptures.

Despite their different origins and dissimilar periods, this eclectic group of sculptures surrounding a drawing forms a bold display of ethnic and contemporary art and craft. The pieces were carefully selected for their contrasting textures and sizes to create a truly compatible composition.

An ebony vulture stands guard beneath a photograph of Rodin's The Kiss – a theatrical combination that is rich in humour and bizarre associations. The heavy wide picture frame prevents the powerful image of the bird from dominating the relationship of print and carving.

There is nothing to keep you from introducing contemporary pieces into such an eclectic arrangement. However, it demands an experienced eye to juxtapose contemporary sculpture with works of art from earlier cultures in order to produce a look that is both natural and elegant. To achieve such an 'eye' you will need to experiment by trying out different arrangements; your first effort is unlikely to be your best. Likewise, the marriage between a single sculpture and a painting or group of paintings in the same room requires careful consideration. In any successful combination, the objects and pictures must be good neighbours. So often, an arrangement will not come together sympathetically because a particular item is vastly superior to the rest of its companions. More with sculpture than other media, perhaps, you may

find that one particular object is just too strong for a room. If this is the case, there is only one alternative: to move it somewhere else.

While the aesthetic criteria used to judge sculpture have continued to evolve, the interest in figurative detail has turned to a concentration on form and on structure, and most recently, to place. In the 1920s Constantin Brancusi was obsessed with the interrelationship between his work and its surrounding space and different light conditions. He photographed his abstract works in different configurations and against dark and light backgrounds to observe the different degrees of reflection off the surfaces. His studies had a profound impact not only on the development of sculpture in the twentieth century, but also on its display in both art galleries and private collections.

The scale and diversity of forms in twentieth-century art, and particularly in sculpture, demands that traditional methods of display be abandoned in favour of solutions where the relationship between the work of art and the space in which it is shown becomes the focus of attention. Hence, the construction of modern living spaces in a variety of configurations – some with Le Corbusier-style planes and curves, others with asymmetric rooms of different heights and proportions – to accommodate and complement works of modern art. Much contemporary sculpture aims to evoke a certain psychological and physical 'world' to be explored by the onlooker; more recently, there have been sculptors who attempt to absorb and control the surroundings: Richard Long, for example, whose large slate circles, which are laid out on the floor, demand minimalist domestic interiors that have been influenced by the designs of modern art galleries.

Consequently, some people prefer to create an atmosphere of museum-like austerity as a background to their collection. Yet, the home-cum-gallery feel, so popular today, is not restricted to those who have a living space that is of a modern, minimalist design. This effect can also be achieved by combining a mixture of bronze sculptures and paintings from this century and before, country furniture, books and bare wooden floors, but in an essentially modern, uncluttered atmosphere. The sparse, light environment infuses the room with an air of importance. The stark perfection of bright white walls and shiny, polished wooden floors discourages the strongest human instinct – the desire to improve.

Because sculpture is three-dimensional, whatever style of design and display has been selected, light will play a significant role in producing a sensitive, natural result. Until light was made available from sources other than candles or fires, sculpture was illuminated by existing natural light from windows placed either in the roof as skylights or high in the plane of the wall, as in many churches, or as rectangular vertical shapes along the outside walls. It was in these spaces between the windows that sculptures from past centuries were often displayed. Natural light was too precious for it to be blocked out by placing sculptures in front of windows. Many of the great Palladian houses in England were designed with long

As well as surrounding a dark fireplace with a range of delicate hues, seen in the painting, sculpture and rug, this collector has gone a step further by playing with shape and form – most noticeably in the way the curves of the figure in the painting are echoed by those of the tall vase-shaped sculpture on the floor.

galleries to accommodate the sculptural treasures acquired by the travelling aristocracy on the Grand Tour. Here, they were set into alcoves, or mounted on wall brackets, and careful consideration of the aspect of light was paramount.

The invention of the electric bulb in the 1880s brought a clean source of artificial light for use in display and transformed the placement of all types of art. Today, the range of artificial sources is vast, as are the methods of illumination, allowing three-dimensional art objects to be shown in all their glory. Directional light will highlight form and reveal surface texture, highly diffused frontal light will cause flattening of shape, and softly diffused, focused light will reveal the sensuous curves of a reclining figure. The combination of artificial and natural light sources presents the collector with the flexibility to display sculpture anywhere in any room, be it the kitchen, windowless hallway or basement bathroom. Unlike in previous centuries, the placement of sculpture in a window is now possible. In fact, for many contemporary sculptures, especially those in which form is of utmost interest, the creation of a silhouetted shape is the preferred result.

Small objects of sculpture present a different problem in how they are to be displayed. A number of disparate and often curious objects arranged together can work as a composition because they are confined by the table on which they are laid out, labelled 'tablescapes' by the English designer, the late David Hicks. The table sets the parameters of the collection in much the same way that a frame holds a picture together and a glass case a collection of stuffed birds. Often in this type of display, it is the colours that are important, a giltwood Venetian rococo table with a dark marble top will contrast with the cream tones in a collection of ivory elephants. Here it is the monochrome quality of the objects *en masse* that makes the impact rather than the sculptural shapes of its individual items.

White walls, floor tiles and furnishing fabric combine to form a neutral backdrop for this impressive collection of South-east Asian art.
The cool expanses of white highlight the creamy tones of the ivory pieces and make a striking contrast with the dark wooden panels and figures.
In a room of such size, the way they reflect the daylight to produce a natural luminance is also very useful.

Poised on tall metal stands, two Balinese figures appear to float midway up a bedroom wall, distracting the eye from the large vibrant painting that dominates the main wall. Among this group of collectables are a Chinese chair, startlingly simple in its design, and a group of red lacquerware bowls on the floor. Arranged at differing heights in a loosely circular formation, each item plays a vital role in this visually stimulating ensemble.

The Natural World

The keepers of Renaissance 'cabinets of curiosities' crammed them with bizarre and wonderful things. Items from their collections often covered every conceivable space within a room, including the ceiling, creating pure magic for the eye and endless challenges for the mind. The many exotic species of flora and fauna made up some of the weirdest but perhaps the most beautiful accumulations and displays of all time, many of which formed the foundations of the world's natural history museums.

Today's collectors display their collections of shells and minerals, stuffed birds, shells or pickled specimens, with the same reverence as collectors of Old Master paintings. While it may take a bit more space and imagination to consider how best to display a fossil skeleton of a Tyrannosaurus Rex and dozens of birds of paradise, the results can be as scholarly or informal as you like.

Though conservation laws now restrict the collecting of some specimens, antique collections of stuffed birds in bell-shaped glass cases, mounted mammals, boxes of butterflies and game trophies can still be found at auctions

Opposite: *The dedicated collector of this assortment of shells has lovingly numbered and separated each shell by type, then arranged them in separate compartments of a drawer. This style is easy to copy for cataloguing and protecting a collection of delicate items.*

Above: *Carefully selected for their unique form and colour, these stones complement the nautical theme of this living space, with its pictures of sailing vessels and porthole-shaped mirrors, to create a clean, breezy atmosphere.*

In this collection is gathered a curious mixture of natural and artificial objects that seems to be inspired by a fascination for the unusual rather than by beauty or craftsmanship. Objects that hail from the sea share space with a collection of miniature models, gathered on the Grand Tour. While their origins have nothing in common, their colours and textures blend harmoniously.

Edwardian ladies placed their collections of natural wonders in glass-topped display cabinets that invited admirers to view the objects from above. However, a tower of shelves allows viewing from all angles and heights, exposing every facet of the items on display. It has been painted a shade of ochre to complement the natural colours of the shells and coral.

and country house sales. Stuffed animals enclosed within glass-fronted boxes or covered with glass domes are usually associated with the 'baronial look' with its accompaniment of leather chairs and heavy wooden furniture that can be found in libraries and gentlemen's clubs. But more imaginative places can be found to display the rich forms and colours of game birds and waterfowl, prehistoric elk antlers, or a preserved polar bear.

For a natural-looking display, birds can be mounted on branches or specimens placed in a reconstruction of their natural habitat that has been embellished with rocks and foliage. At the other extreme, a sculptural display of birds or other eye-catching specimens can be made by arraying them over an entire wall. The arrangement can be made even more informal by mixing it with other elements, such as boxes of butterflies with decorative birdcages. Even paintings can be intermingled.

In the entrance hall, the stairwell, kitchen or dining area, cased specimens can be placed in neat, graduated pyramids or in geometric patterns, or, if the specimen is particularly stunning, it can be displayed on its own for maximum impact. Hang an object above the bed, sit one on your sofa, let another dangle over the kitchen table, and no one will fail to be captivated by your eccentric spoils. Driven enthusiasts may choose to display objects in every corner of their house.

Collections from the natural world may include objects as exotic as crocodile skulls, fossilized bear skulls or cases of parrots, but many prefer to embellish their homes with more delicate collections of pressed flowers, dried leaves, specimens of seaweed, iris tubers, heaps of pebbles or phials of coloured sand that have been collected on their travels. Such objects are widely collected but can be hard to display. Presenting these specimens *en masse* is one

The intimacy enjoyed between collector and collection is clearly evident in this extraordinary bathroom, alive with birds either soaring ceiling-ward or perched against a wall. Luxuriating in the antique rolltop bath provides one with an excellent position from which to observe these splendours, or from which to stretch out an arm and retrieve a cherished book. Antique taxidermy and books usually conjure up dust and gloom but here they bring an ordinary space to life.

The eighteenth-century Swedish naturalist Linnaeus used scores of botanical engravings to cover the walls of Hammarby, his home
near Uppsala. Here, the method has been reinterpreted with a subtle difference. Instead of placing the engravings edge-to-edge as Linnaeus
did, the sheets of paper have been spaced apart deliberately, in order to highlight each pressed plant.

way to make sure that they have an impact. Pressed dried flowers or leaves can be stuck down on paper and then fixed to the wall in the manner of wallpaper in a stunning celebration of nature, and yet by arranging furniture in the room as you would normally, the display becomes casual rather than overwhelming.

Collectors of stones and shells are known for their laissez-faire attitude towards their finds, though sometimes the informal presentation detracts from the beauty of the objects. Seashells suffer the most in this respect. Amassed in great numbers, they are often relegated to huge bowls or dismissed in piles on shelves within cabinets, where all too often, the beauty of each individual item becomes overwhelmed. Larger shells, however, go wonderfully with ancient art, and can be displayed to great advantage on bookshelves, between the books and along-side stones or classical fragments.

Stones can become sculptures in their own right when they are placed on tabletops, either on their own or next to contemporary sculpture that echoes their shapes. Collectors who choose to display them in a cabinet should beware – collections of stones have a habit of growing at a pace that is beyond belief. Be sure to have your cabinet designed in such a way that it can soon have a mate to stand or sit nearby.

Fish or anatomical specimens preserved in glass jars filled with alcohol may not appear to be promising objects for display, that is unless you want to establish a museum of taxonomy. But, arranging them together and identifying the specimens with handwritten labels of black ink on white paper can make a surprisingly dramatic display. The impact of such an arrangement will depend largely on the background colour of the shelves on which they are placed. Grey is an excellent choice, as the objects them-selves will add enough drama without the need for a vivid colour. You can form a composition that consists of a group of bottles that are all of different sizes and shapes – for such an arrangement the actual colours of the specimens are less important as the bottles themselves are the focal point. Here, the act of collecting may conflict with the art of display, for those who prefer to arrange their specimens in an orderly scientific manner will seldom produce the most artistic display.

If you are one of the many conservationists who prefers to serve as a guardian for nature's treasures, you can sketch these noble objects and display your rendering instead. This may sound like an unlikely proposition, but an old fishing lodge near the island of Skye in the north-west of Scotland (illustrated on page 35) demonstrates how life-size paper depictions of giant sea trout can become the most dominant feature of an interior.

Pages from an eighteenth-century herbarium set in gilt and wood box-frames decorate the walls of the dining-room in a château in Normandy. Suspended candles, birds perched on wrought-iron hooks and an 1830s crystal Baccarat cage may seem unlikely neighbours, yet combine perfectly when displayed, as here, with imagination.

Ethnographic and Folk Art

The temptations offered by the vast range of objects categorized as 'ethnographical' means that the homes of those who collect ethnic art can quickly become extremely cluttered; there always seems to be the need to acquire just one more Polynesian fish hook. After the fish hooks, it is a stone adze, and after the stone adze, just another mask and after the mask, a shield. It is not long before canoes and totem poles are being contemplated. Incidentally, if you do find yourself succumbing to a totem pole, the stairwell is just the place to put it. Like the early collectors of exotic foreign 'oddities', contemporary connoisseurs of ethnographic objects provoke surprise by the unexpected juxtaposition of extraordinary and varied items. As crowded as such rooms may seem, however, nothing will have arrived in its place by accident – the positioning of every object, sculpture, shield and painting has been carefully planned.

These multifarious displays work successfully, as any collector's home or museum display will show, especially if trouble is taken to construct distinct areas within the room. It helps to divide the room into sections and compose each on its own before stepping back and viewing the room as a whole. This way, you create separate readable elements that hold the eye's attention and stop the room becoming one massive display with no focus. Smaller collections of objects always seem to work best on tables,

Opposite: *A collection of Guerro burial masks, mounted so that they jut out from the wall, lends excitement to this room. The drama is continued by the early collections of American hunting implements and Egyptian and Thai vessels that have been deliberately arranged to jostle for space on the shelves.*

Above: *The positioning of this vast collection of art and minerals may at first appear to be disparate, however the highly charged colours and distinct organic shapes of the objects have been carefully chosen for the striking contrasts they produce.*

and the addition of items such as fossils, minerals, bowls and glass objects to the ethnographical items will help to carry your eye around the surface with ease.

Though colour is seldom the major consideration when forming collections, paying attention to colour and detail helps to avoid a jumbled effect. Grouping objects by colour and shape is one way to arrange a large display in a homogeneous way. However, placing objects of strikingly different colours next to each other can create a stunning contrast. For example, you might consider alternating the dramatically brighter tones of beadwork or ceramics with the more subdued colours of wood or basketry.

Arranging wood masks or beaded objects by type is also an option. Ethnic objects of similar aspect and origin seem, in many instances, to have far greater impact when shown together. Shields, spears, clubs, masks and African figures benefit from the effect of being in a group. A melange of 30 or more terracotta burial masks mounted closely on a wall can make a really effective display despite their bland colouring, especially if they are mounted at various distances from the wall to add dimension. Similarly, collections of flints, shovels and pottery vessels can be arranged *en masse*.

When ethnographic pieces are displayed in this manner the background does not really matter, as the strength of a coherent collection overcomes the effect of position. For example, a display of 20 or so Polynesian figures arranged on the lower steps of a contemporary marble staircase does not look out of place, whereas one or two single figures might. While the power of a massed collection of ethnographic art can sometimes overwhelm other elements in a room, large quantities of ethnic art, mainly because of the influence that it had on many of the great painters and sculptors during the first half of this century, can often benefit from being juxtaposed with modern and contemporary paintings and artefacts.

Opposite: *Natural light from a nearby window bounces off the vivid blue interior of this custom-made display unit, creating jewel-bright cubby holes for this collection of Meso-American figures. The display succeeds in transforming what might otherwise be a bland stairwell into a source of delight.*

Top: *The intersecting lines on this mask from the Punuh tribe in Gabon create geometric shapes that are mimicked by the alternating triangles of coloured beads on the flasks.*

Bottom: *Placing a collection of indigenous masks at the end of this galley-shaped retreat creates an illusion of width and a memorable image. The impact of the display would be lost if the masks were aligned.*

Setting ethnographic objects, like traditional African dolls, alongside Western or contemporary pieces, such as china dolls or even art deco jugs and teapots, creates an engaging contrast. One may choose to use rough wooden shelves and ledges to set off the light wood of the African figures or to highlight the display of the more brightly coloured Western pieces. You might even use a single colour as a unifying theme for the arrangement of starkly

Stairs are ready-made permanent display spaces, particularly useful for large groups of objects of varying height and shape, such as this collection of African figures. This group occupies the lower steps of a staircase; a larger collection, however, could be taken all the way up to the top.

different objects. This will give the display a feeling of completeness as well as demonstrating the importance of a varied use of colour.

Often a collector is attempting to make a personal statement about his collection in the way it is displayed. A prize possession might be singled out and shown on a plinth or pedestal, in a window opening or in a separate, deep box-like recess. Shelves made with a box effect (see page 84) are superb for compartmentalizing a collection, while at the same time emphasizing each individual piece. For greater effect, the insides of the boxes can be painted a cold, deep blue or red, making an especially striking background for both monotone and multicoloured objects. At the same time, the definition of the box implies that these pieces are not to be touched, that they are meant to be observed from a distance. Artificial light, especially from fluorescent bulbs will always add an atmosphere of formality, and perhaps harshness, to a display, while natural sunlight will produce shadows and reflections, giving it a warmer and friendlier appearance.

A much more inviting feeling emanates from ethnographic objects that are laid out haphazardly around the room or on a shelf in front of rows of books. This kind of display encourages you to pick up the objects and look at them, turn them over in your hand and put them back again. Setting these kinds of objects amongst books is an easy way of suggesting that they are there to be touched and examined, for books like almost nothing else, exude an air of friendliness. A visitor left alone in the room would feel no inhibitions about touching the artefacts displayed like this in much the same way he or she might take out a book to read while waiting for their host to return. A warm, softly coloured background that does not correspond to particular pieces will encourage this more relaxed response to the items in a collection, as neither the position of each object nor the sense of the display itself is emphasized.

Although embellishing walls and shelves with a mass display of ethnographic items will make a compelling presentation, simple displays are equally powerful. Folk art is an area of collecting especially suited to this type of display. In this category, the greatest proponents of simplicity are the Shakers, who collect very little except what is essential to their functional way of living. Reducing their furnishing to the very minimum, the Shakers have been an inspiration to many of the leading designers of the twentieth century, and their furniture and means of its display are widely copied. The best way to display Shaker furniture is without ornament and as far away from most other types of furniture as possible. As for their chairs, of course, you could follow the Shaker

fashion and hang them upside down on a pegged rail. This austere approach to display can be successfully applied to ethnographic and other folk objects as well. Small wire hooks, hidden nails or discreet picture rails help to draw attention to the object itself rather than the means of support. On such a pared-down background, the objects are the focus of the room and nothing interferes with the power of their presence.

A vast array of American folk art and musical instruments is ingeniously displayed against white walls in this suitably rustic setting. The late nineteenth- and early twentieth-century instruments blend harmoniously with the tower of Shaker boxes because of their similar colours and textures. The shop storage unit, contemporary American naive paintings and a rooster weathervane further embellish the room with rural charm.

Textiles

Textiles are associated with nearly every part of our lives, and their stunning colours, boldness of design and sensual textures are ideal for creating dramatic and enveloping displays. Yet, the very act of displaying them can be detrimental to the fabrics themselves. Whether the textiles in question are contemporary knitted fabrics or traditional rugs, light should be a major consideration; it causes dyes to fade and the fibres to become brittle. Finding a compromise between display and protection is the answer.

One way to preserve textiles on show is not to reveal the entire piece. Colourful ethnic fabrics or embroidered silks piled high in an open cupboard make a chic display that can be closed off at will. You can mix styles, periods and materials, and the open arrangement will invite the curious viewer to root out any example to have a closer look at its workmanship. Alternatively, Indian textiles, quilts, art deco fabrics, or even Aubusson tapestries can be laid over deep armchairs, tables or sofas in layers of contrasting colour, making an unusual covering. Used in this way, only a glimpse of each piece of material is on view, protecting the unseen areas from light damage. Rotating the layering of the pieces will also avoid uneven patches of colour as the fabrics fade. Obviously, however, fabrics used in this manner are not immune to the everyday hazards of spilled drinks and muddy feet.

If you are not prepared to take a risk with your textiles, you can frame them just as you would frame a picture under glass. Box-frames work well for uniforms, costumes and oriental robes, but position the framed fabrics to avoid direct sunlight. Far from making them less interesting, displaying these rich fabrics in darkened parts of a home emphasizes their fragile beauty, and placing them in half- rather than full light greatly increases their sense of drama. Delicate pieces such as woven Indian silks and screen-printed cottons are easier to hang if they are first sewn onto backing fabrics (see page 169).

Once they are made ready for hanging, collected pieces can be placed almost anywhere. Framed African Kuba cloths make a high-tech, stainless-steel kitchen more personal. Quilts, in particular the American patchwork ones, Navajo rugs, Chinese priests' copes and Turkish kilims

Above: *Running the risk of fading and soiling exotic fabric is a small price to pay in comparison with the drama created by hanging and draping them. The owner of this bedroom has turned Indian appliquéd cotton roof-cloths into a canopy over the four-poster bed and richly textured blankets into curtains. Wrapping, looping and layering are other dramatic ways of displaying fabrics that do not require careful preservation behind glass.*

Opposite: *The entrance hall in the late Rudolf Nureyev's sumptuous Parisian flat demonstrates his faultless attention to detail. Elaborate neo-classical paintwork, elegant black-and-white tiles and a collection of fine paintings temper his more theatrical touches, such as hanging costumes from the 1966 production of* Sleeping Beauty *on an antique mahogany coat stand.*

Do not rule out the idea of jumbling together miscellaneous objects, such as these shawls, baseball caps and vases, if they have something in common. In this case, everything is identically coloured. Bold colours, such as red or yellow, or various tones of the same shade work extremely well; a theme that can extend to other objects positioned nearby, such as furniture and works of art.

Brightly coloured textiles, arranged in neat stacks according to tone, pattern or method of manufacture, achieve a patchwork effect when contained within a closet. The eye-catching bundles – including fabrics in brightest fuchsia pink, lime green and banana yellow – lie together in complete accord. A row of colourful bottles along the top of the closet intensifies the exhilarating arrangement.

look startlingly original suspended like tapestries from curtain rails, draped in a hallway, or hung against a wall as a backdrop for a bed.

If richness and romance are the effects you desire, patterned textiles from Russia, India or southern Europe in a plum or red room, with dark wooden shutters or plush velvet curtains, create a luxurious atmosphere. Fabrics often look best when used in quantity. Their tactile qualities can be shown off to their greatest advantage by juxtaposing fabrics of different types, draping them across tables or chairs to reveal the contrasting textures.

Those more interested in the craftsmanship and detail of, for instance, American Indian garments, with their colourful quill and bead decoration, might prefer to

display them against a light-coloured wall for greater emphasis. You may wish to arrange textiles of this type alongside hand-made pots and woven baskets in a suitably rustic setting. Yet the strong visual elements of such pieces will work perfectly well in homes where the architecture is elegantly understated, such as the haciendas of southern Spain. Similarly, Japanese robes and teacups suit an austere background, while robes displayed with their arms outstretched take on a sculptural quality and stand out beautifully in a modern context. You may very well want to focus attention on an individual piece, and by taking it away from its usual setting and displaying it in a less likely location you will create a striking visual surprise.

As with ethnic artefacts, textiles can be arranged by colour and shape and combined with other complementary pieces from a collection: for example, African carvings seem to mimic the curving lines in the patterns of Persian rugs, and kindred spirits can be found in Indian shawls and brilliant oriental brocades. By marrying similar elements – vertical or horizontal motifs and colours – you can achieve natural and unforced combinations.

Many people, however, are uncomfortable with formal styles of display, and prefer a means of showing off their collections that is more relaxed: rolls of Turkish and Kurdish kilims that have been tucked under a bed so that only their tips can be seen; an obi that has been casually draped over the back of a chair; theatrical costumes hung almost haphazardly one on top of the other on a coat stand; or perhaps a group of flags leaning in the corner of a room. It is, in fact, all too easy to underestimate the amount of effort required to create such a display, so do not be surprised to learn that someone has thought long and hard about the exact composition of such groups. In many cases, it is the seemingly casual effect that takes the greatest amount of thought to achieve.

Imagination and flair have been used to arrange this collection of textiles, covering walls, floors and furniture and creating a totally coherent space. Individually, the chair is aesthetically pleasing, as is the rug or the robe, but grouped together they create a far more stimulating display. The kaleidoscope of pattern, colour and texture produces a room of provocative beauty and visual interest.

Ceramics

Above: *Although porcelain remained popular in the mid-eighteenth century, its method of display had evolved since the 'china mania' of the previous century. Services that had once sat upon wall brackets or over chimneypieces were now contained in cabinets, often of oriental design, with or without glass fronts. The various-sized compartments and shelves of this tea cabinet offer a wide choice of positions for an extensive collection of blue-and-white china.*

Opposite: *The juxtaposition of objects of contrasting colours, textures or size can provide particularly effective displays. Here a row of small jewel-coloured glazed beakers creates a repeated pattern above a giant Greek oil jar, accentuating the larger vessel's voluptuous curves and textured patina – a stunning illustration of how simple ceramics can make eye-catching displays.*

While many people fall prey to the charms of ceramic dinner services, tiles and figurines, few are lucky enough to have grand cabinets to house their collections. There are, however, all kinds of alternative ways to display these colourful or monochrome pieces, ranging from the simple to the utterly flamboyant.

Genuine collectors possess a scavenging instinct which endows them with the ability to find a precious item among a mass of dross. Collecting a piece at a time like this will give you a unique dinner service – one of odd plates and bowls. Such a service is called a harlequin set and the possibilities for assembling these are endless. For a harlequin service to become a thing of beauty it is important that each piece relates to the others. This relationship can be one of matching colours, design, shape or even texture. In fact, it can be as mercurial as a piece having the same feel as its companions. Once you have amassed a number of pieces, you can take immense pleasure in creating order out of what may have seemed like a group of disparate items. This will require a creative skill that appeals directly to all collectors – the impulse to make patterns.

Do not dismiss rustic shelving: heavy timbers surrounding delicate china makes a stylish combination, their strong colour contrasting with the delicate hues of the glazes. Alternatively, highlight the unique characteristics of individual pieces by displaying them on their own.

If open shelves do not appeal to you, try using an antique or modern bookcase to house your collection. Paint the bookcase white to provide a striking backdrop for various colours, shapes and sizes and arrangements. Flea markets and salvage companies are good hunting grounds for tall glass-fronted school cabinets, which are ideal for displaying a collection of plates, saucers and jugs in disparate colours. Stacking plates rather than standing them upright can have an abstract, sculptural quality which will enhance the collection of treasures.

Obscuring part of an object is often a good way of provoking curiosity and interest. For example, you could make a chic but tantalizing display by placing a collection of teapots on shelves hidden behind translucent sliding fabric screens or Japanese-style partitions covered with layers of hand-made paper. They will provide diffused light and control ventilation at the same time.

Contemporary ceramics of technical virtuosity and poetic strength – like these by British artists Lucie Rie and Bernard and Janet Leach – demand uncluttered space. Plexiglas shelves, with a silver-leaf back panel, provide a light-filled, reflective showcase for this mixed group.

Salvaged from a school sale, these seasoned cabinets suit perfectly the display of Russel Wright dinnerware in period colours. More valuable ceramics would sit just as comfortably in this setting as the units are rich in colour and classic in design, allowing a variety of different styles of ceramics to be shown in all their glory.

Sometimes the type of ceramic will determine the place and kind of display. Dining-room walls are an obvious backdrop for exhibiting ceramics. This is the area where you would traditionally find blue-and-white pieces of early Ming or later reproductions. In the seventeenth century there was a great vogue for blue-and-white export china, and in England, Queen Mary was at the forefront of this collecting mania. Chinese *kraak* porcelain, teasets in brilliant blue and white were highly sought after as well as imports from Japan and these were used to make immensely beautiful decorative compositions. Masses of these pieces were displayed in and around fireplaces, in pyramidal overmantel arrangements and in cabinets. With its strong yet subtle decoration, blue-and-white china looks wonderful against either a distinctively coloured or white background. It is often mixed with plain white, celadon or even polychrome pieces nowadays, and is still seen in arrangements on top of cabinets, or hung on the wall with invisible brackets. Another variation on the traditional presentation, however, is to use dishes and bowls to frame a doorway, or even to fill a 'dead' area of a room. Ceramics suspended from hooks on the wall can be easily re-arranged or moved to accommodate new arrivals.

Displays of the past can teach us much about the successful ingredients of porcelain display: attention to detail, colour and the placement of objects. One of the most famous and remarkable displays devoted to collections of ceramic objects is the pleasure salon at Oranienbaum, commissioned in the early 1770s by Catherine the Great of Russia, to house a series of figures

A collection of odd china teacups and plates – ready for use at the first opportunity – sits very happily in this hand-crafted cabinet. Inset into the wall and void of any extraneous decoration, the simply designed cabinet is a showpiece in its own right but does not detract from the dazzling pink, blue and yellow hues of the china.

from the Meissen factory. It is one of the world's finest examples of a room that has been specially built to house such a collection, the swirling rococo decoration in sympathy with the prancing horses and heroic figures that sit on gilt-and-white consoles.

Charles III of Spain was crazy about porcelain, too. His obsession was spurred on by his marriage to Maria Amelia of Saxony, daughter of the King of Poland, who had set up the first European porcelain factory at Meissen in 1710. Charles later set up a factory in Capodimonte, in the hills above Naples. In 1757 he built the Queen a small salon decorated entirely in porcelain, with brightly painted parrots and dragons perched and curled on gilt porcelain baskets of fruit; even the candelabra were covered in monkeys, snakes and fighting birds. The room was punctuated with mirrors linked by ribbons of pink, pistachio green and purple.

Although these exquisite, whimsical royal rooms are not to everyone's taste, the ostentatious gilt stucco ceilings, specially made gilt consoles and the placement of mirrors, together perfectly convey a feeling of luxury and sensuality. However, creating a monochrome room featuring only blue-and-white pots placed on brackets entails just as much thought and attention. You will need to consider the spacing, type of display used and choice of furniture and floor coverings, as well as where to site mirrors. You may want to accentuate the collection with another decorative element, such as flowers. These final touches often have little to do with the pieces concerned, but they can have a great effect on the overall success of the display.

Ceramic tiles are nearly as popular with collectors as dishes and figurines because of their spectacular colours and designs, but they are much harder to display. Using them as they were originally intended – to decorate walls, floors or ceilings – seems to present the most satisfactory solution. Set them into the risers of a staircase, embellish an entrance hall, or for the sheer splendour of it, cover a whole wall with a collection of tiles. While this has the great advantage of carefully preserving the tiles, it makes for a permanent collection and is not recommended for those who expect to move house. The celebrated painter Frederick, Lord Leighton was so fond of his collection of Islamic tiles that he created a fully tiled room for their display, the spectacular Arab Hall at Leighton House, London.

Although displays of ceramics work particularly well when they are arranged *en masse*, because of their bright glazes, rich patterns and organic shapes, they also sit splendidly on their own. Whether you choose Plexiglas cubicles, robust stone shelves or platforms of glass suspended by wire in an undulating pattern (see page 146) to show off your collection, the overall effect will be strong and certainly not boring. Ceramics by such twentieth-century artists as Pablo Picasso and Jean Cocteau display extremely powerful graphic images that can make a real impact when they are exhibited singly on a pedestal. Just as wonderful are different-coloured ceramic bowls or individual figurines carefully positioned on a shelf. Regardless of whether it is on its own or set up to contrast with other, less bold, elements in the room, a display of well-chosen ceramics will inevitably provoke the excitement that is the very essence of collecting.

This collection of round dishes by Pablo Picasso features the artist's obsession with bull fighting. The powerful graphic images set against a terracotta background give the ceramics great presence; the white lines around the edges of the plates suggest ranks of spectators. The set lends itself equally well to being hung like a series of fine paintings as being placed on pedestals like sculpture.

The undulating shapes of these black Etruscan vases make powerful outlines against a white wall and a monochrome print. The display area itself could not be simpler: a plain wooden platform shows off the group to perfection. Any additional enhancement such as flowers would compromise the effect of this display.

Glass and Mirrors

Natural light sets the bright acid colours of these frosted glass Murano bottles ablaze. Their position in front of a window ensures a continual burn of colour and quickly draws the eye to the table. This living room would be notably subdued without such an eye-catching collection.

Light is a key factor in the display of glass. The visual impact of glassware is determined by its opacity and by variations in light. Brilliant sunlight will pass through translucent glass objects and be diffused through its surface, creating a spectrum of beautiful effects. Coloured glass will glisten with fairground brilliance in bright light; lower the light levels and the mood will change accordingly. Dark-coloured glass radiates an intriguing moody feeling because of light's inability to pass through it. Interspersing glass bottles and bowls with cream pottery

will exploit these different effects to the full, emphasizing the contrasting translucent and reflective qualities of each material. Collections of common glassware on a dark wooden dresser might fail to stand out, but the occasional exotic glass object, such as an unusually long-necked vase or colourful vessel, will add sparkle to what might otherwise be a mundane display.

One of the most remarkable collections of glass is at the Rosenborg Palace, Copenhagen, housed in the Glass Cabinet built in 1714 for King Frederik IV of Denmark (illustrated on page 51). It is probably one of the world's greatest collections of seventeenth- and eighteenth-century glass, much of it manufactured in Venice. Although at first it appears to be an extraordinary clutter, this is an enchanted maze filled with masterpieces of the glass-blower's art. Pyramids carried by *putti* holding knives, forks and spoons of glass, are combined with mirrors and glass in all forms and colours. The designer, Gottfried Fuchs, created a grotto-like room true to the baroque idea: extravagant, whimsical and at times slightly vulgar. The glass is both the decoration and the reason for that decoration.

Such an overwhelming and fanciful assemblage, however, is not every collector's aim. Using heavy wood shelving instead of glass invites a striking contrast between the thick wood and the fragile glass items. The heavier elements will convey a feeling of great security and solidity rather than fragility. Still, you may prefer the delicate look of glass items on glass shelves, despite the risk of disaster that working with glass can sometimes bring. You can also use box-style shelving to isolate individual pieces that are particularly striking in their design and colour.

In contrast to more artistic methods of display, there is something very attractive about glassware that is presented as if it is ready for use. No matter whether it is a tray of jugs or a trolley of glasses and vases, it is the utilitarian aspect that is part of the charm. Glasses of all sorts work well arranged together, with a great rarity hidden amongst the turmoil. Displayed in this casual manner, the exceptional piece will quickly draw interest once the observer starts looking carefully at the arrangement. Anyone with an 'eye' will spot the star piece in a moment.

Top: *Shapely cocktail glasses, twizzlers and tumblers dating from the 1950s form a dazzling array of glass on a curvaceous metal serving trolley. The harmony and balance of this display is achieved by the combination of various heights and shapes, punctuated by bright splashes of colour.*

Bottom: *The beauty and brilliance of both clear glass and crystal is intensified when placed on a reflective surface. Light bounces off the intricate facets of these jugs and pitchers set on a mirrored tray, to dazzle and trick the eye.*

Below: *An entire wall devoted to a display of glass breaks up the monotony of a private study, giving the occupant a focus for thought and reflection. The glass has been arranged according to colour, shape or size – sometimes contrasting, sometimes matching. Light plays an important part in the effect of this display, altering the radiance of the pieces as it changes direction and intensity.*

Opposite: *Displayed against a window, the pieces in this collection are lit up by day to create the effect of a three-dimensional stained-glass window. Colour appears to pulsate through the objects, fading and growing in intensity throughout the daylight hours. The curves of the glass and clover-shaped leaded designs on the window create a symmetry of pattern that further heightens the visual impact.*

Much like those who look in them, mirrors come in all shapes and sizes. The earliest examples were made from polished jet, bronze and other metals by the Greeks, Romans and Chinese. Jan van Eyck's famous painting *The Arnolfini Wedding* of 1434 is probably the most famous image demonstrating the magical quality of mirrors, but glass mirrors as we know them today were uncommon until the sixteenth century.

It is the shape and, more importantly, the design of the frame that helps to identify a mirror's period of manufacture, but age is not the only quality that attracts collectors. Mirrors with elaborately carved or mirror-plated frames, mirrors on walls, or set in alcoves, ceilings and occasionally, floors, all capture the collector's eye. Though they come in myriad forms, their purpose is universal – to reflect an object or a person, create the illusion of space, or to reflect light, in other words, to deceive the eye. Unlike a collection of paintings or sculpture, mirrors hung together may have little relationship with each other, and their effect depends mainly on the scenes and light they reflect.

Mirrors seem to belong foremost in the bathroom – shaving mirrors, dressing mirrors, harshly lit make-up mirrors – but displays of mirrors can be far more daring. The mirrored reception chambers in baroque and rococo palaces represent the best known examples of extravagant displays. In these grand spaces, mirrors often covered entire walls or were placed at strange angles, intermingling with portraits or reflecting porcelain figures. Nowadays, covering just one wall of a sitting-room with a collection of mirrors in all sizes and shapes produces an intriguing atmosphere. No pattern or symmetry is needed: allow your imagination to run wild and marvel at the result.

Some mirrors, like one hung in a drawing-room over the fireplace, seem to find their place out of habit, but these can actually serve an additional purpose. Apart from enlarging the sense of space, they reflect the reverse side of any china jars or figures arranged on the mantelpiece. Concave or convex mirrors have always seemed best placed in a library, adding to the scholarly atmosphere because of their odd shape and properties. These eyeballs of glass, which catch a room in microcosm on their swollen surface, are most effective framed in ebony or tortoiseshell and hung from heavy silk cords.

Glass and mirrors work well when arranged alongside artefacts of the same period, for example, 1930s chrome-mounted mirrors used to reflect furniture from the same era, or painted bottles arranged to cast tints against a nine-teenth-century patchwork. Such items can be used to complement each other, hold the display together and exploit the reflective and translucent qualities of glass through contrast. The trick in creating a successful display with mirrors or glass is to set the magic in the material free.

Above: *These crystal doorknobs display a range of intricate, multi-faceted finishes. To show off each individual surface to best advantage, some pieces have been arranged lying on their sides – for a change in perspective. As light strikes the finished display, it refracts and reflects within each piece to create a rainbow of colours.*

Opposite: *Mirrors permit light and space to flicker and float, creating a sense of continual movement as images loom to and fro. When you hang a number of mirrors together the possibilities to create illusions seem endless. If the collection includes a number of different styles and designs, so much the better, as the mixture of curious shapes and contrasting ornamentation will make a striking display.*

Metal Objects

From the humble to the rarified, the range of metal objects sought after by collectors is endless. Utilitarian items such as hinges, keys, locks, bells and all kinds of vessels can be as satisfying to track down as pieces of higher value, most notably those from eastern cultures: Chou dynasty bells, Japanese swords and gold beakers from Ur, for example, which find their way into more specialist collections.

Serious collectors of metal objects find as many attractive items in the backs of furniture restorers' or carpenter's shops or along river banks as they would in auction houses or in antique shops. The quality of the collection is, as always, a reflection of the collector's eye rather than their purse. In some of the better collections the star items have cost little or nothing. Moreover, in the very best collections there are no star items – it is the way in which individual items have been brought together that determines whether the collection succeeds or fails, and this is as true for the most common items.

A collection of keys found in a garden shed or bits of rusty pipe picked up from a beach, for example, may seem unlikely candidates for collecting and displaying. But in these cases, the arrangement of the display itself – perhaps a velvet-covered panel, or a brightly painted wall – can transform them into objects of beauty. Found objects have particular appeal because they represent a secret passion in collecting; they have a personal connection,

Left: *Plain wooden shelving provides a pale, textured backdrop to contrast with the sleek dark lines of this candlestick collection. The candelabra are positioned at strategic points in the display to create a balanced, almost symmetrical pattern. A dark metal shelving unit would lessen the impact of this display considerably.*

Below: *Arranged according to their size, equal rows of metal keys graduate from small to large in this simple graphic display. Everyday objects of little value may lack beauty or visual interest as individual items, but en masse create surprisingly decorative two-dimensional patterns. With practice, arrangements such as this one can transform the most unlikely collection of items into a work of visual brilliance.*

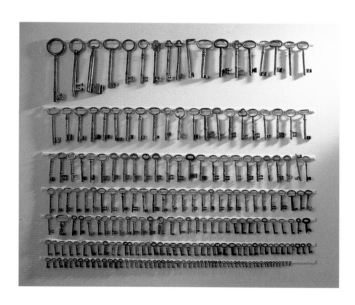

Low wooden tables, characteristic of oriental simplicity, make fitting display surfaces for these Chinese bronze vessels.
Presided over by a life-sized Buddha elevated on a platform, this impressive display – the focal point of the room – is uncharacteristically
numerous in terms of the typically austere preferences of the East for the single object, yet nevertheless imparts a tranquil atmosphere.

evoking memories of holiday walks and surprising finds. It is usually preferable to hang such items on a wall or arrange them on tables rather than placing them in cabinets, as they have little of the intrinsic value we associate with items placed in the exalted and protected setting of a cabinet. Many collectors of found objects like to have them where they can be touched and handled, perhaps on a work desk or dressing table. These are objects that

will move from home to home and remain with the collector along the journey to wealth or the fall to poverty – for some, they are the icons of their lives displayed upon personal altars of existence.

For a successful display of metal objects, it is not just a matter of putting the objects in the correct room. How you arrange them within the room is also important, and for that there is no single formula. Metal objects, however,

*Weathervanes fashioned from sheet metal in the shape of horses, roosters and cows drift above a shelf crammed with plates,
jugs and implements in this eclectic display of countryside treasures. Against the neutral, cream-coloured wall, the animals seem to come to life,
and the plain background highlights their distinct grainy patina acquired during years of service.*

more than those made from other materials, do have
an innate strength that is conveyed most effectively in
simple, accessible displays.

One system for found objects is to place them as they
arrive in your collection and then, as needed, move them
about until you achieve an arrangement that is visually
satisfying. The rarer and more valuable metal objects can
be displayed with the same reverence as any piece of
sculpture or fine porcelain. Sometimes it is better to resist
placing weighty objects on stands or mounts, as they
generally seem more at peace lying directly on the surface
of a table or floor without any encumbrances. Such a
Zen-like atmosphere does not in any way suggest a lack

of respect for the objects; on the contrary, a display
that has a sense of serenity can be eye-catching, indeed,
even dramatic. Beautiful bronze Shang vessels or
Vietnamese drums placed on a long, low plank of wood
make a strong statement and will immediately become
a central feature of a room. More delicate pieces, however,
are better suited to being arranged on shelves or even
suspended from the wall.

If you desire a busier atmosphere, then mass collections
of items as diverse as candlesticks, bronze Napoleonic
columns, or hunting horns of all shapes and sizes, can be
arranged across a table or mantelpiece, where the surface
texture contrasts with the metallic quality of the entire

Set inside a custom-built bookcase, this framed glass vault makes an ingenious display case for a precious collection of ancient bronze and jade objects from China and Central Asia. Like the surrounding books, the antiquities have been arranged vertically and horizontally to create an intricate pattern. Although the case acts like a magnet for the eye, other delights, such as the Tang horse and Asian pottery placed between the books, commingle brilliantly.

group. For magpie collectors, who are always wishing their display space were just a little bit bigger, it is constantly necessary to discover new ways of displaying their truly cluttered collections. Lateral thinking is required to produce bold and successful displays for quantities of pewter spoons, brass padlocks, corkscrews and keys. Every surface should be considered, for often the backs of doors, sides of shutters, and even the outsides of cupboards can be utilized. Shelves can do double duty, too: it is just as easy to hang items from the underside of shelves as it is to place objects on top of them. It it important to remember, however, that for the best results the scale of the metal object should correspond with the display area around it.

One of the most remarkable and appealing qualities of metal objects is their patina, whether it is the bright sparkle of polished copper, the dark glow of bronze or the aged chalkiness of verdigris. All these materials are enhanced by the wooden surfaces and pale colours characteristic of minimalist rooms, but they look equally at home in richer surroundings, where deep greens, reds or browns can complement their various sheens. The importance of an appropriate juxtaposition of materials cannot be over-estimated: heavy padlocks placed directly onto glass shelves would make for an uneasy arrangement, but a small velvet pad placed between the crude lock and the sophisticated glass shelf will provide the necessary balance.

Tools and Household Implements

Above: *Always choose a shelving system that is in sympathy with your collection. Graphic wire echoes the decorative patterns of 1950s black-and-white ceramics in this bold composition.*

Opposite: *Having filled every available shelf in a pantry, the owner of this collection of enamelled teapots, coffee pots, milk jugs and pitchers has created extra storage space by hanging handled items under the top shelf as well as from the ceiling. Hanging items provides an unusual perspective, allowing each piece to be viewed from various angles, rather than from one side alone.*

Seemingly ordinary objects can become works of art, but not everything that has either been found or made by human hands will fall into that category. The fact that a collector has chosen an object for its own particular properties – whether it is a jelly mould, garden tool, or kitchen utensil – imbues the object with a unique quality that makes it something apart. Although originally made for everyday use, tools and household implements have been rediscovered for their craftsmanship, use of colour and design. When we look at them in this way, we recognize that many of them are objects of great beauty. Derived from their honest utilitarian aesthetic, their functional forms provide great potential for use in imaginative displays.

The familiar, basic shapes of kitchen ceramics – teapots, pitchers, soup tureens, mixing bowls and plates – can take on another dimension when arranged *en masse*. Examples of mochaware decorated with geometric or dendritic patterns, spongeware with its characteristic mottled designs, or even the most simple of monochrome pieces, can make distinctive compositions. Some of these kitchenware items are classic collectables – for example, the clean, sculptural shapes of white-glazed ironstone pottery, first produced in Staffordshire, England, in the 1840s and later in America. However, most types of crockery are collected regardless of their style. It is the solidity and colour of kitchen ceramics that make them so well suited for display anywhere in the house.

We are used to seeing traditional collections of complete dinner sets or parades of several dozen teapots kept on the open shelves of a wooden dresser in a country kitchen. By taking advantage of the shapes and colours of these pieces, it is possible to achieve more imaginative and contemporary displays. Using a block of intense colour as a background for plain white forms provides a stark contrast that will give them an almost abstract quality. Coloured pieces, too, can benefit from a backdrop of a contrasting shade. A collection of ironstone gravy boats on dark, heavy, wooden shelves set against a brightly painted wall is suited to a farmhouse kitchen, but will infuse the room with a slight air of modernity; shelves painted to match the colour of the background will fit in with the style of more overtly contemporary kitchens and allow the objects to stand out.

Equally effective, but more relaxing, is a display of white ironstone plates placed against a background of pale pink or light lavender. These lighter shades give both the room and the collection a mellower atmosphere. The same collection can be made to work in a wide range of settings: rustic chinaware displayed on rough-hewn pantry shelves looks homely in a country kitchen, whereas on smooth white surfaces it has a clean functional look that can easily be integrated into a contemporary environment.

The graphic forms of many architectural, household and farm tools beckon collectors to take advantage of their display potential, be they cast- or wrought-iron implements, such as spades, kitchen trivets, sickles and scythes, or more elaborate hand-forged tools, decorated with heart motifs and gentle hooked curves. Arranged either in a single line, or massed against a cool coloured wall in a softly lit space, their distinctive forms will appear almost like silhouettes. In bright daylight a group of these shapes will make a more striking and powerful image.

Although these objects may seem ordinary on initial inspection, looking closely one discovers the originality in the ingenious shapes of shepherds' crooks, rakes, long-handled pruners or elongated spades. Within each of these categories, there are literally dozens of variants: garden spades, for instance, produced for different functions sport distinct shapes. Some heads are curved, others rectangular; some are pointed at the tip, or concave. Their length means that they lend themselves to vertical display, whether hung on a wall in an entrance hall or up a stairwell. By staggering the spades, rather than aligning them, you can create an aesthetically pleasing composition out of hitherto functional objects. The rhythm of the display can be further enhanced by punctuating it with related objects such as a workman's hat, a pair of gloves, or other tools.

One problem with collecting farm implements is the scale of some of the objects you might wish to display. A keen collector of American farm tractors decided, after filling two large sheds, one old barn and three outbuildings with these big, bulky machines, that he wanted to make his collection more accessible. The semi-circular cast-iron seats proved to be pieces of art in their own right and consequently inspired him to remove them from the tractors and mount them in rows against the light grey-coloured timbered wall of his workshop. When daylight streams through the barn door, the cut-out decorations and lettering throw enlarged shadows against the rustic wooden surface, creating a display of great charm.

Some utilitarian objects have been collected for so long that it is easy to forget that originally they had a more important role than mere decoration. Throughout history woven baskets have been used extensively by almost all cultures for everything from fish traps to fruit holders, for cheese-making, water-carrying and as goose covers, which were placed over the heads of the birds while their feathers were being plucked. The more standard shapes continued to be used for carrying eggs, shopping or a picnic.

For the collectors of baskets, it is not only the fascinating shapes that catch the eye, but the texture and patterns that are produced by the different weaving methods and

Above: *Cream shelves provide a neutral background for this striking mass of green Depression-era glassware; a large painted metal laundry bowl makes an inspired container for kitchen utensils.*

Opposite: *Floating like icebergs in a sea of glacial blue, this group of nineteenth-century ironstone jelly moulds demonstrates how traditional objects can be used to create a contemporary display.*

enormous variety of woods and grasses to be used in their construction. The size and shape of the baskets, the weaving designs, lacy patterns and rough textures are all considerations to be taken into account when selecting a method of display. A collection of shallow hexagonal openwork baskets made from wood strips can be hung facing out from a wall washed with a colourful glaze, the colour providing a contrast to the basket's neutral hues. Equally, they could be hung on hidden hooks or Shaker-

style pegs against a neutral ground to ensure that the baskets themselves are the main focus – rather than any background colour or texture. The coiled baskets produced by the American Indians of the Southwest, which are notable for their cultural and artistic – as well as their utilitarian – qualities, are a prime example of striking patterns and colours. Their lively designs and earthy colourings, ranging from orange reds to rich reddish browns, inevitably provide the starting point for any

arrangement. Derived from naturally occurring pigments, their colours generally complement each other, even if their patterns and shades differ. Like other tools and kitchenware, they can be skilfully arrayed against a background of a harmonizing colour to make a vivid display that is both sophisticated and pleasing.

The beauty of workmen's tools and implements from centuries past is inseparable from their original humble purposes, be that tilling the soil, carrying eggs or baking bread. Over the centuries, tools and utensils have been modified in shape to improve their function; they have been decorated with designs to suit their owners; and they have been made from ever more technologically advanced materials. For the majority of people, however, they are still considered everyday objects. In rediscovering them, and by taking the time to appreciate their workmanship, simplicity and variety, we are finally giving them the place of honour they deserve.

Opposite: Shepherd's crooks, jostling for space along a wall, lend a pastoral air to a formal entrance hall. The unaligned vertical crooks create an undulating pattern, broken midway by the addition of a leather shepherd's hat. The baskets below have been displayed on their sides to save on floor space and offer an unusual view. Positioning the two collections one above the other emphasizes their obvious connection.

Above: A conventional picture rail supports various architectural instruments, including callipers and compasses. Their distinct, repeating shapes dance against the pale yellow wall, echoing the sculptural forms of the chairs below. This picture of symmetry draws on the similarities between disparate objects and is the result of hours of precise positioning. Artfully, a mirror's reflection becomes the central image.

Toys, Models and Miniatures

The display of toys, models and miniatures is largely dictated by their Lilliputian scale. Toy soldiers, dolls, dolls' furniture, model boats and aeroplanes may be small in size, but they are full of character. Their individual charms can be easily overlooked or overwhelmed in any arrangement that is too massive or unsympathetic.

Toy soldiers, for instance, are often seen laid out in battle formations on a table or in regiments on shelves, but neither method is particularly satisfactory when it comes to showing off the individual pieces at their best. Nor, for that matter, is it advisable to position them in front of books on shelves, as these small vertical pieces will be dominated by even a row of books. A more effective way

to arrange them is in a wooden box with numerous compartments – like an egg crate or a typesetter's letter tray. Here, the brightly coloured soldiers can be examined individually and the unique properties of each can be fully appreciated. From a distance, the pieces will form dots of colour creating an effect that is reminiscent of a pointillist painting, blending into one another in the viewer's eye to make a greater impact amongst other items in a room.

Unlike lead soldiers, dolls and their furniture vary widely in size and shape. One must always consider their different forms and materials when displaying them. Keeping pieces in a doll's house is one obvious solution, but dolls' houses, too, tax the display talents of collectors. A doll's house removed from a nursery and placed in a sitting-room ceases to be a child's toy and instead

Opposite: *Collectors of miniature objects often present their collections so that individual pieces can be selected for closer inspection. These miniature chairs can be picked up and moved about whenever the desire arises. Part of the enjoyment of ownership comes from having control over a small, perfectly formed world.*

Above: *Executed with panache, this extraordinary display of antique miniatures stands out against an emerald green wall. The collection includes architectural models and chairs from England, Italy and Spain supporting Chinese and Japanese dolls. Hanging objects against a vivid backdrop creates a composition that defies the imagination.*

becomes simply an object to admire. Despite its change of circumstance, and as it still contains evocative and powerful memories of childhood, it can live perfectly well in a sophisticated room.

Sometimes the collection of furniture has outgrown a single doll's house and either more houses are needed or the decision has to be made to extend the display into the room. The tops of low cupboards and bookshelves can be utilized for a parade of tiny furnishings, the books giving weight and stability to the fragile items sitting on top. To make the composition more interesting, some of the tiny chairs can be tacked onto the wall in miniature Shaker fashion. With a collection of several hundred pieces you may end up with shelves running right around a room; if you choose this arrangement, the shelves should be narrow in width to keep them in scale with the furniture. Once again, it is the arrangement of the shapes and colours of the individual pieces in the collection that will make a success of such a display. If there are several of the same item, such as chairs, each to a different scale, it might be a good idea to group them together, so that the smaller versions are not lost and the idea of scale itself becomes a point of interest.

In general, dolls are collected on a considerably larger scale than dolls' house furniture. One way to present a collection of dolls from many countries and in a range of styles is to hang them against a suitably coloured wall. Use fishing line tied around their waists and attach it to a hook fixed to the wall to ensure that each doll is fully visible but safely secured. This method is particularly helpful in displaying unstructured dolls such as American rag dolls, which vary dramatically in shape and size and are notoriously limp. However, dolls standing alongside or sitting with other curiosities and artefacts of modern living, such as stereos and compact discs, can be arranged to produce an eclectic but harmonious composition. Here, too, it is important to consider the doll's size and shape when deciding how best to arrange the collection, as they need to appear large enough not to get lost among other objects.

Mechanical tin toys can be effectively displayed in both individual and compartmental settings. Once again, a large wooden shelf arrangement resembling an egg crate works well for the smallest examples. Shelving will contribute more to the display if it has a rustic appearance, recalling the origins of folk art and the simplicity of childhood objects. Furthermore, the use of contrast – in this case, the rough wood meeting the metal or plastic finishes of the toys – adds textural interest. Bigger items can, of course, be positioned much as any other piece of art, either singly or arranged on larger shelves or tables. The juxtaposition of objects of different scales excites the eye in a way that a collection of objects of the same size often does not.

An aspect of display that is rarely considered is the perceived – as opposed to the actual – weight of objects. This is particularly important when considering collections of miniatures. Souvenir buildings and miniature monuments are made from both heavy metals, like bronze and lead, and lighter zinc, tin and aluminium – even moulded in glass or resins. However, those made from the lighter materials should be placed anyway on a solid, weighty shelf to convey the appropriate feeling of strength expected of a foundation supporting full-sized versions of these structures. Objects that look heavy can seem uneasy when placed on glass shelves and appear more at home on more substantial settings, such as wooden tables and desks.

Opposite: *Suspending marionettes from a chain tacked to the wall provides the perfect solution to accommodating a constantly growing collection. The only drawback is that this idea is bound to encourage further acquisition so that the display continues around the room, then leads into another, only ending when the entire house has been filled.*

Above right: *The addictive pleasure of collecting drove the owners of this collection of 2,400 miniature models to convert an outbuilding on their California estate into a dedicated showhouse. More than 100m/ 300ft of shelving teems with the towers, spires and domes of both real and imaginary buildings. In addition to the vast array of architectural gems, there are numerous architectural prints by Piranesi.*

Right: *Few toys have been made in as many varieties as the doll, which is why serious collectors end up possessing hundreds of examples, even if they concentrate on just one type. Doll enthusiasts, therefore, have to be prepared to expand their collections. These articulated wooden religious figurines stripped of their finery appear to be frozen in position but can be moved at any time to make way for new dolls. They can also be manipulated into a variety of different poses to give the entire display a totally new look.*

Metal plinths set these faithful replicas of airships apart, showing off their individual qualities to the full. Taking time to assemble a small collection of superior items is far more rewarding than quickly amassing many mediocre pieces, as this display shows. The owner of this collection has chosen the simplest method of display against the plainest of backgrounds. A strongly coloured or patterned background would distract the eye and mixing the collection with disparate objects would certainly diminish the impact of the group.

Once a suitable surface is found, the models can be arranged in a number of different ways depending upon which qualities you most wish to highlight. You might arrange models of buildings in imitation of their real-life setting, with streets running between them. When arranging small objects, however, it is important first to plan a composition and then consider how the composition will fit into the room as a whole, always taking care to maintain the overall balance.

Another display trick is to present the collection so that it is partially hidden, either high up on shelves or in a half-opened cupboard or drawer. This idea also helps to resolve spatial constraints when large collections of toys or miniatures need to be accommodated. Semi-obscured objects always inspire a sense of curiosity and discovery. It is not hard to imagine a collector standing on a chair and fetching down some great rarity to show to a fellow enthusiast. Such a display can also encourage the viewer to touch and hold the objects in their hands rather than merely look at them.

If money is no object, the means of display can be as elaborate and detailed as you like. Collectors of model boats and toy soldiers could even attempt to replicate the unique displays of the publishing magnate, the late Malcolm Forbes at the Forbes' Magazine Galleries in New York. He was keen to show his objects as they might have been used by children, so toy rowing boats sit playfully in bath tubs, submarines appear submerged and toy ships sit placidly on clear Plexiglas. Because he believed that his collection of 10,000 soldiers needed to be infused with life, revolving stands were installed so that the regiments parade before you as if marching to the beat of a military band. While this is a highly effective, if complicated and expensive way to show a vast collection, an undeniably large part of the joy of collecting toys and models comes from their intrinsic ability to capture the imagination. This can be true of even the simplest displays. For the serious collector of toys, dolls, trains, boats, marbles or soldiers, far more modest arrangements will elicit just as much pleasure, for the imagination will supply the rest.

Soaring and swooping like miniature acrobats on brightly coloured trapezes, toy figures and painted balls create an animated scene across a ceiling. The coloured cords from which the models hang crisscross at bizarre angles adding to the sense of movement. This imaginative presentation brings the toys to life, offering the viewer a scene of pure entertainment. It is a performance frozen in time, reminiscent of the one that amazed Gulliver, given by the little acrobats on tightropes in the beguiling land of Lilliput.

Personal Collectables

Personal items of clothing or accessories are often collected with the same relish as priceless art, and the displays they create can be even more fascinating. The late Duke and Duchess of Windsor were among the most avid collectors of personal memorabilia. They took as keen an interest in their domestic surroundings as they did in their immaculate appearance. The Duke's collection of leather-bound volumes was arranged in red-lined book-shelves and his day shoes placed in serried ranks in his dressing room. The Duchess collected priceless jewellery as well as pug pillows, which sat at the bottom of her bed.

Collecting the latest couture creations or timeless vintage clothing has always been popular, but recently the vogue for collecting these items has reached an all-time high. At auction, cast-offs of the famous regularly fetch prices that are equivalent to those attained by the work of world-renowned artists. It appears that some second-hand clothes and contemporary creations have acquired the status of 'art objects'. Suddenly, the question is: do you wear it, or do you hang it on the wall? The answer is: both. Hung directly on the wall or in a frame, an article of clothing becomes an artwork that is a cross between a painting and a sculpture. Devoid of human presence, clothes are flat, formal and almost abstract in shape, and many are immensely beautiful. Artistic and tailoring talents can sometimes be better appreciated off the body – hanging a pleated garment of translucent fabric against a window, for example, allows light to enhance its compli-cated structure. However, a passionate collector of clothes will still take every opportunity to wear their most original and desirable pieces. Clothes come to life when they are worn, transforming them into kinetic sculptures.

The accessories worn with clothes can also work their way into artistic collections. Peggy Guggenheim was not only passionate about collecting dogs, but almost every-thing else as well, including modern paintings and the men who painted them. Her keen eye also perceived the sculptural potential of exotic earrings. These she displayed in her bedroom at her palazzo in Venice, symmetrically placed on either side of the fireplace and affixed to the walls in a carefully considered fashion.

Opposite: *Period lunch boxes have been lined up on kitchen shelves to form an unconventional display of television celebrities' faces. Big, chunky items such as boxes, biscuit tins and bottles may seem rather ordinary individually, but once arranged together in a suitable position in a kitchen or living room, they make an arresting spectacle. Like all collections of ordinary practical objects, this assemblage becomes more interesting and sophisticated each time a new example is added to the group.*

Below: *Preserved for posterity or collected purely for pleasure, detach-able shirt collars make a surprising personal display, evoking a bygone age. Stacked one above the other on wooden poles behind glass, theirs is a seemly form of retirement after years of starch and wear.*

Personal items, such as hair combs, fans and antique hand mirrors, are often displayed in private spaces, such as the dressing room or bedroom, and are there mainly for the enjoyment of the collector. The key is to have enough items to make a convincing display, even in a limited space. The same is true of a table carefully laid out with sewing, smoking or writing implements. What seems at first glance to be a pleasantly cluttered table will reveal itself to be a carefully arranged still life. Beautiful compositions seldom happen by accident.

When creating such arrangements, particularly with personal items, it is helpful to have a structure around which to work. By placing objects around a doorway or a dresser you can form a frame that adds interest to an often under-used space. Surprisingly, the empty spaces between the pieces can be an important part of the display. The sculptor Henry Moore once held up his hand and asked his companion what he saw: 'Fingers,' was the reply. 'No,' said the artist, 'I see the space between the fingers.'

It must also be remembered when displaying personal items that there is more to these objects than just their aesthetic quality. They are the repository of our memories and associations. The cowboy hat evokes the swaggering hero portrayed by John Wayne or James Stewart on the big screen. The tired old pair of boots or gloves are a reminder of days spent enjoying the great outdoors.

Arranged in sculptural stacks, these American Bakelite radios from the 1930s and 1940s form a wall of technology encased in plastic. Collections of everyday domestic appliances, particularly models from these and later decades, are sought after because of their distinct design features in stainless steel and moulded plastics and as historic examples of technological progress.

Boots, like other items of footwear, are best displayed at foot level, on a floor or on the steps of a staircase. Accordingly, the collector of this sprawling collection of cowboy boots displays an obvious enthusiasm for heavy footwear by monopolizing an entire corner of a room with the collection. The distinct shape and weight of the boots make this a powerful spectacle.

Hats hold a great appeal for collectors. Even if they are crushed and tatty, they look well displayed in a group, either hung on a wall or piled high, one on top of the other. One collector has hung cowboy hats around the top edge of a bathroom wall, interspersed with cowboy ties to imitate a traditional egg-and-dart cornice. Arranged together, cowboy hats, ties and boots form an evocative tribute to the Wild West. And who would have believed that old boots could make a fine display? The worn-out boot, however, has all the qualities of human contact that collectors and decorators look for today. Their patina and wrinkles of age are impressive in the right setting, whether they are hung by their laces from a beam, or arranged in rows in a hallway. The strength of their impact depends upon the size of the collection: one pair of boots hung from a long beam would look as if a builder had left them behind by mistake, but 20 pairs make a statement.

Cowboy boots are a either a tough necessity or a flamboyant accessory. They are best presented in a way that emphasizes one of these qualities: either viewed from above, as they are on the foot, or seen from the front or side where the stitching can be appreciated. Ideally, they should be displayed on the floor, as their rugged looks demand a solid base. They also look particularly good lining a staircase because the graduated levels allow several pairs of boots to be successfully displayed at once.

Displaying women's elegant high-heeled shoes requires a totally different approach. Placing them alone on a table or a mantelpiece, or even on wall brackets in the manner of porcelain figurines, creates a boldly effective display. The shoe can be elevated to an even higher level of artistic merit: set in a box-frame or on a single pedestal and placed, like fine sculpture, in a picture gallery or entrance hall. For decades London fashion designer Vivienne Westwood has made shoes of such innovative shapes and designs that they have even been acquired by collectors and museums.

The list of personal objects that appear in collections is endless. Collectors of men's clothes might also amass ties or stiff collars. Ties displayed haphazardly over a rail, just as they are kept to be used, is easily accepted by the viewer's eye. Displayed out of context, even the bow tie can become an art object, and a display of these can echo the feeling of a modern painting, even though its constituent parts are all rather old-fashioned. Collars might be placed in neat rows in a glass cabinet like a collection of stuffed birds, giving the feeling of something long dead. Like those who enjoy ties, pipe-smokers tend automatically to amass collections of pipes, simply because they never throw an old one away, perhaps keeping their arrangement on a desk where they can change the pattern daily.

Whether you collect pipes, earrings, hats or dresses, when it comes to displaying them there are two basic alternatives. One is to place the objects in context, like putting cowboy hats and boots together on an old trunk. The alternative is to remove the context completely so that they are isolated from their past and purpose taking on instead the feeling of the abstract or surreal – the display is a work of art in itself. Either way, the display can be as individual as the 'eye' that produced it.

Stylish accessories offer collectors all the appeal that makes the world of fashion a glamorous place. In this elegant living space, a column of sunglasses decorates a narrow slice of wall, with the air of a surreal artwork.

The principal element of a pleasing display is the repetitive use of a particular shape. Here, in the heart of a collector's bedroom, tortoiseshell combs are arranged in the shape of an arch round the top of a mirror, mimicking the curve of the fireplace.

A treasure trove of finds from flea markets and photographic galleries may appear to the uninformed eye as a collection of kitsch memorabilia. In fact, this group of objects has been carefully selected and superbly assembled by a collector with an impeccable eye for colour and form. Each and every object has a particular place in this setting: photographs by Diane Arbus and Leon Borensztein sit comfortably in the cabaret-like atmosphere of this very personal collection.

Display Techniques

COLLECTORS PERPETUATE THE JOYS of collecting through their chosen methods of display. The German architect Mies van der Rohe said: 'God is in the details', and while it is essential to think about the overall style of your display, it is equally important to pay close attention to details – be they the size and shape of frames and mounts for your prints, a marble or bronze base for your wooden effigy, or how best to play with light and shadow. The main aim is to unite all the essential components of the display – the practicalities and composition – in such a way that together they create a new and harmonious space for you to experience and enjoy. Successful displays, like the objects in your collection, are works of art in their own right.

In the following pages are described some of the simplest, yet most effective, techniques for creating successful displays, many of which will give you the confidence to start experimenting with ideas of your own. Perfecting these methods takes time and a certain amount of patience, but it is well worth making the effort when such innovative and individual displays can be the reward. Although there will always be certain limits to displaying objects in terms of their size, shape or colour, you can still be creative within those limits. If your first few attempts do not produce the effect you had in mind, then rise to the challenge, and look at it from an entirely different angle. Dismantle the display, rearrange it, or if necessary, relocate the collection altogether. Persevere until you are pleased with what you see. The end result is the work of your imagination, so the measure of its success will be entirely subjective.

Collectors consciously or unconsciously select objects that will 'fit' with the others in their collection. In some cases the need to complete a collection dictates the choice, however, it is often how the object will be seen in relation to those around it that provides the motivation. Will the new item dominate the collection or merely act as a support within the group? Sometimes it is simply a matter of whether their sizes and shapes are compatible, whether they fit visually. Besides aesthetic compatibility, a collector will often use an intellectual or emotional motive for including an item in his or her display.

Opposite: Dynamic displays defy convention, mixing cultures and styles with grace and ease: a simple chalk drawing framed in elaborate gilt; an Indian print shown off on a carved wood Indian bookstand; ancient terracotta pots perched on white marble capitals; a collection of ties draped over a Japanese obi stand – the trick is to ignore obvious partnerships and dare to make an unlikely match.

Putting a collection together is about setting a scene and creating an atmosphere. You might place a collection of vases in a red lacquer Chinese armoire lit with soft ambient lighting, or treat a group of miniature chairs like modern sculptures, placing each on an individual plinth. In the same way that an artist uses light, colour and texture, each object should provide a focus and induce wonder and resonance. The strength of a group or a solitary object should engage the eye and arouse the senses, not just because of the objects themselves but because of the way in which they are arranged.

Successful displays require an eye for practicality as well as beauty. Considerations such as securing and hanging pictures, selecting the right size of plinth or the correct type of cabinet or shelves, are crucial. Whatever it is you are using to support the bulk of the display must be strong and sufficiently safe as well as pleasing to the eye. Without looking too heavy, picture rails, for instance, be they brass, bamboo or cord, must be sturdy enough to carry the work of art. Glass and other unstable objects should be secured to surfaces with microcrystalline wax or carefully weighted down with sand to keep them upright and safe. Another tip for mounting objects is to insert a moulded resin pad between the base and the object to keep it secure and protect it from damage.

Lighting, an essential component of a display, has its obvious safety risks, too. Make sure the lights are positioned at a safe distance from the objects on display to reduce the risk of fading and heat damage, and avoid using high levels of lighting altogether if any of the materials within the display, such as delicate fabric or paper items, are light sensitive. For aesthetic and safety reasons, tuck the cabling carefully out of view and conceal unsightly switches and controls, where possible.

Thinking about small details can prompt the creation of an entirely new look or a revamp of a jaded display. Sometimes even minor adjustments to the objects in a display can allow you to show them off from a new perspective, or reveal features that were previously hidden. Plates, for example, can be hung by attaching adhesive discs to their backs. Alternatively, they can be placed on mounts with adjustable tabs that allow you to tilt the plates at an angle on shelves, or provide support if they are hung on a wall. Clothing can be padded out with unbleached, undyed fabrics or mounted on custom-made mannequins. Brass rods can be soldered into 'T' shapes for wall or table mounting, or a 'spider' shape with three crossbar arms, to support dolls, stuffed toys and other items of a complex shape. Often, these rods are covered in clear flexible tubing to protect the objects on display.

When the finer details of a display are faultless they tend to go unnoticed, but a single unsightly feature can mar the illusion you are trying to create. However, with foresight and a little ingenuity, these problems can be avoided. For example, ordinary window glass has a greenish tinge around its edges because of iron contamination, which tends to make warm colours appear grey. Bear this in mind when you next have something framed and ask the framer to use iron-free glass, if possible, to avoid any colour distortion.

Experimenting with the positioning of light sources can make all the difference. To prevent unwanted glare and reflection on shiny objects, you can reposition the light source to produce indirect or angled light.

Be wary of your limitations: sometimes you will need to call on the expertise of professional mount-makers, framers, cabinetmakers and installers who are aware of collectors' needs and the safest, most up-to-date methods of display.

Practicalities and professional expertise aside, it is often those who dare to take risks who produce the most spectacular combinations. Being adventurous enables you to manipulate form, colour and shape and may produce elegant, composed results. Odd pairings create delightful surprises: a leather motorcycle jacket hung on an antique Japanese kimono stand, for instance, or a cluster of political badges pinned on to a denim jacket and hung against a wall. There is no need to splash out on expensive display units. A deep wooden table topped with a sheet of glass makes a good showcase for beaded couture handbags.

And for the less timid, simplicity and generosity of spirit are two key points to bear in mind when it comes to showing off a collection with style. When in doubt, keep the display simple; go for the understated mount, frame, plinth or cabinet; then add a twist. As William Penn, founder of the Pennsylvanian community of Quakers, said: 'Frugality is good if liberality be joined to it.'

Frames and Mounts

Framing an image or object enhances its beauty, its aesthetic form and the power of its message. Without a means of containing the composition, these qualities may be lost. A frame separates the work from its surroundings, focusing the viewer's attention. While frames have a practical purpose which is to protect, it is their power to enhance the visual and symbolic interest of an image or object that is their greatest asset.

Styles of hanging vary and the style you choose can influence the overall mood you create. Hanging a series of framed pictures in a straight, even line evokes the formal elegant style of hanging, typical of the eighteenth century. Alternatively, hanging a mixture of pictures in frames of different sizes in an asymmetrical arrangement recalls the styles of the 1960s.

Mounts, too, play a significant role, particularly as far as drawings and watercolours are concerned. The colour, tone and width of a mount are all critical considerations. A mount also ensures that the paper is stretched taut and lies flat so that there are no wrinkles when the image is covered with glass. Like frames, the type of mount you choose depends on personal taste and fashion, but you may also be influenced by the intended setting for the frame. Whether your choice is simple or elaborate, the goal must be to complement the picture, not to overpower it.

Originally, paintings were limited to icons or frescoes that were fixed permanently to their surroundings. However, with the Renaissance came the possibility to possess pictures as moveable commodities; the European frame was born – as ornamental and lavish as the painting it was designed to surround. Elaborate ornamentation, ranging from painted foliage to carved scrolling, was used to embellish the architrave or *cassetta* frames that were popular during this period. All the principal guilds of craftsmen played their part in the design and manufacture of frames, including the cabinetmakers, who designed frames in the same way as windows or door mouldings. These simple architrave frames, hung together as a group, initially became popular because they harmonized well against a tapestried or panelled wall.

For centuries, frames have been subjected to the whims of fashion just like any other form of decorative furniture. For example, *trompe l'oeil* was used by the Dutch portrait artists of the seventeenth century, while French painters of the same era preferred to present their work in elegant frames carved in giltwood – masterpieces of furniture in their own right.

From the mid-nineteenth century to the present day, major European artistic movements have yielded a stream of highly original designs. In the 1960s, large Abstract Expressionist canvases were very seldom framed, not merely because of prohibitive cost; many artists considered a frame to be superfluous because the work was

Sophisticated framing services take advantage of computer technology to help their clients choose the perfect frame and mount. A photograph of the picture is scanned into the computer and shown in various styles of frame, allowing the client to view all the available options. The service speeds up the decision-making process and helps prevent costly mistakes – far easier than choosing from a few corner samples of mouldings in a limited range of colours.

Below: *Fan collectors often display the objects from their collections in boxes made of thick plywood bent into the classic arched shape of the fan. Each open fan is sewn to fabric and stretched over a backboard. Shaped glass is placed in a groove at the bottom of the frame to protect the fan from dust. Plexiglas stands and holders can be used to support these beautiful objects in a variety of positions.*

Opposite: *Three-dimensional objects are often difficult to hang on a wall without some kind of support. These heads have been crudely fixed to painted wooden frames to enhance their appearance and provide a means of support. Some items, such as raised embroidery, require a shadow box frame where the glass is placed between the inner and outer frame and thereby raised, away from the surface.*

deemed to be complete in its own right. Howard Hodgkin took a rather different approach, sometimes extending his brushstrokes over the mouldings surrounding many of his works, making the frame part of the composition.

Generally, it is best to choose a frame that suits the style and period of the subject matter. However, deliberate mismatches can lead to astonishing results: an abstract painting showcased in a seventeenth-century carved gilt frame is bound to cause a reaction. Similarly, an Old Master in a modern frame would be equally arresting. Mismatches such as these demand skill and too often are unsatisfactory. A successful partnership between a painting and a frame, however, can be immensely inspiring.

Try not to concern yourself too much with whether the newly framed painting will match its setting. It is far more important to make sure that the frame and painting complement one another, rather than focusing too closely on whether the frame will match the curtains or wallpaper.

Consider first whether the picture actually looks better in a frame – it may not need one at all. Then, if you decide the picture will benefit from framing, decide on how elaborate the frame should be. Try and achieve some kind of balance between the subject and frame, so that one does not overpower the other. Take particular care with small paintings as it is easy to choose something that is too heavy or decorative. While a single picture may benefit from a ornamental frame, a series of pictures so framed and hung together could look disastrous.

When you acquire a new painting, it is tempting to rush into framing the work as soon as possible. However, give yourself time to get used to its colour and vibrancy. Watercolours and prints are a different matter. Framing them is a way of securing the glass that protects them and keeps them in place. These frames should be as simple and unobtrusive as possible. Heavy frames could dominate their delicate brushstrokes and soft shades.

Paintings are often sold already framed. Where possible, it is better to leave the frame with the dealer and only take the painting, the only exception being when the frame is part of the painting or has been designed by the artist. These frames should not be parted from their paintings. Naturally, if you disagree with the artist's choice, do not be afraid to reject the frame and choose your own.

This portrait of William Shakespeare by John Taylor
(c.1610) arrived at the National Gallery, London, in
1856. Since then the portrait has been on display
in a number of strikingly different frames, including
an eighteenth-century Maratta frame (top left), and
the overpowering mock-seventeenth-century frame by
prominent Victorian frame-makers Foord & Dickinson
(top right).

During the 1950s or '60s the portrait was placed
in a simple glazed box with a velvet background.
Then in 1983 it was reframed by John Davis in an
old tortoiseshell frame (bottom left), not unlike its
original, which successfully enhances the scale of the
portrait and complements its colours.

The Dutch artist Frank Visser found an ingenious way to house his collection of tiny found objects by hanging a series of frames tightly together on a wall to create a miniature Venetian loggia-style display. Each of the frames contains a mount cut into eight individual arch-shaped niches. To force the eye inwards, Visser chose mouldings with rippled edges. The bevelled edges of the recesses are outlined in gold to enhance the objects. The use of identical frames and the tight hanging formation creates the illusion of a larger decorative space.

An asymmetrical jigsaw arrangement makes a good display solution for a disparate group of photographs, such as these. The mix of frames – black, white, metal and wood – works well because they all have a classic white museum-style mount in common to unify the group. The odd one out – the porthole mirror, just off centre – adds an element of surprise and humour. Several pictures have been left unhung, tempting the eye to roam through the display and find each one a home.

Surrounding a painting with a mount before it is framed can completely transform its appearance. Like frames, mounts come in various styles, capable of creating a whole range of different effects. Delicate watercolours, for example, benefit from having a mount because it provides a certain amount of distance between the painting and the frame. The choice of colour and the type of mount used depend entirely on the painting in question.

Strong twentieth-century watercolours and drawings seldom need anything more elaborate than a plain white or off-white mount. Romantic watercolours and drawings of the nineteenth century are often improved by a mount

with thin, coloured lines echoing the shape of the frame and picking out a colour in the work. These lines help bridge the sometimes awkward gap between mount and picture.

Drawings from the Renaissance, often in light, coloured chalks benefit from darker mounts which guide the eye inward, while Persian miniatures shine out from highly decorative silk mounts – the simplicity of their colours contrasting wonderfully with the complexity of their mounts. Decorative mounts can be made by covering plain acid-free board with velvet or antique wallpaper, or hand-drawn decoration in ink, pastels or watercolours.

Right: *Using a mount to display a watercolour, drawing or print provides a restful space between the work and its frame. This elaborate mount in French yellow board surrounds a seventeenth-century print. The layers of overlapping mount form steps towards the print, encouraging the eye to focus on the detail of the subject matter. A wash of colour has been painted along the edges of each mount to form a series of inner frames around the image. The contrast between the royal blue gilt frame and yellow mount produces a fittingly regal effect.*

Below: *Items that have something of interest on both sides, such as a letter of historic value or a watercolour torn from a sketch pad, can be secured between two sheets of glass and displayed on a stand so that both sides can be viewed. Not all items require the protection of glass, however. These inexpensive decorative prints are shown to great effect on classic wooden plate stands, set on the shelf of a bookcase. Music stands and miniature easels are just as effective for showing off even the most modest of prints.*

Plinths

Sculpture and other three-dimensional objects often need plinths or stands to be fully appreciated. Even when an object can stand freely on a table or shelf, a plinth draws a visual line between the object and the display surface, giving it special prominence.

The trick is to find a plinth that complements the virtuosity of the work without unbalancing the harmony of its proportions. Ormolu bases became the vogue for showing off pieces of oriental porcelain during the reign of Louis XV, their decorative qualities providing the perfect match for their elaborate subjects. Nowadays, fashions are simpler. But although contemporary bases may be less ornate, they can still be elegant in their simplicity and choice of materials: small wooden bases, covered in silk brocades or velvet make excellent bases for small gold boxes, silver cups or bronze figures and at only moderate expense. Ethnographic objects work well on boxes faced with hessian and linens in beige, brown or black. Choose a plinth or stand in a colour that complements the piece: white marble on black granite never fails to impress, while brass objects mounted on green or black marble is another popular choice. Experiment with a variety of bases of different heights, widths and colours to see which works best.

As with framing a picture, setting an object on a plinth requires some consideration. You will need to decide on the height and angle of the support. With sculpture, it is often helpful to determine this by studying features, such as the spacing between the eyes of a bust, the dimensions of the piece, and its colour and weight. In addition, you may need to consider a sculpture's original perspective: for example, a gargoyle would be viewed from below.

The subject to be displayed will determine to a large extent the shape and weight of the plinth. A tall, cylindrical object, such as a totem pole, will need an equally tall and perhaps thin but strong support, while a heavy sculpture often demands a weighty base of marble or granite, or a substantial mahogany pedestal. Consider whether the object should stand freely on the plinth or be fixed to it in some way. It is not always necessary to attach an object to its base. However, in cases when support is needed, some objects can be drilled and fitted with a metal dowel or held in place by metal or Plexiglas clamps, while others may be attached so that they can rotate.

Sometimes one object in a collection can be used to display others. Upturned capitals of ancient columns make fine pedestals for large modern pots; jewellery can look spectacular when mounted on a collection of mineral samples; a home-made plywood table covered in a tribal textile makes a colourful support for silver bowls. It should not be necessary to spend a lot of money on a base: originality is the secret of good display.

Opposite: *Painted and stained wooden bases of different heights support giant rock crystal, wood and stone balls which once graced a* Wunderkammer. *A group of identically shaped items can be made to look more interesting by varying the height and space between them. This enables the collector to highlight a superior specimen by standing it above, or apart from, the rest of the group.*

Below: *Small and elegantly proportioned, these giltwood stands show off a pair of ivory portrait discs to perfection without detracting from their intricate beauty. Slotting the bases of small items like these into a carved groove attaches them securely and prevents accidental damage.*

Creative contrasts make displays such as this rough-textured bust perched on top of a smooth plaster base even more memorable. Other unusual touches can be added too, such as placing the whole composition on top of a stack of timber squares. To break the symmetry, angle the squares slightly to produce a jagged edge. Novel supports like these add a witty note to an otherwise formal display. Try using modelling stands, terracotta drainage pipes, chimney pots, concrete wedges, railway sleepers, books, or even slabs of smooth-edged glass stacked at various angles. These inventive and resourceful methods of display are often more eye-catching and affordable than conventional bases and stands. Odd juxtapositions of textures and types of materials can work, but experiment first until you find the perfect combination.

Left: *Unobtrusive Plexiglas and metal stands temper the mood of these ethnic wooden masks; the combination works well in a sleek modern interior. Most mounting specialists tend to prefer compact minimal display stands; however, a heavy square base made of tropical wood or black marble, in keeping with the carving's earthy origins, would work just as well.*

Below: *Proportion is essential when it comes to displaying sculpture, but all too often it is misjudged. The stand supporting this large plaster head is just large enough to achieve a balance; any shorter or narrower, and the composition would fail. Painting the stand a darker colour makes it appear heavier and provides contrast. A strong stable base and a secure means of attachment are vital. Metal gallery stands which are adjustable in height are often an excellent choice, although many collectors prefer wood or marble.*

Cabinets

Like the collections they contain, cabinets have always been prized for their construction and handsome lines or, in the case of early examples, for the rarity of their decoration, whether ivory, lapis or gold. Described by William Morris as 'the blossoms of the art of furniture', cabinets antique or modern, grand or modest, have always been coveted pieces of furniture.

The first cabinets, such as the one in the Palazzo Medici in Florence, were actually small intimate rooms, often situated next to a private study or bedroom. A French dictionary of 1632 describes a cabinet as 'a closet, little chamber or wardrobe wherein one keeps one's best,

or most esteemed, substance'. These were places where princes could contemplate their treasures in peace, whether vessels made of semi-precious stones or collect-tions of cameos. It was not until the second half of the seventeenth century that the word 'cabinet' was used to refer to a piece of furniture.

As tastes and fashions in collecting changed, so the cabinet used to display them evolved. Rudimentary boxes for storing and transporting valuable items were made in Spain in the early sixteenth century. These chest-like cabinets, later known as *vargueños*, had hinged front flaps which opened downward to reveal an array of small

A dedicated collector of pebbles commissioned a cabinetmaker to construct this fine wooden cabinet to hold his collection. Categorized according to size, colour or place of origin, the pebbles are arranged on shelves and in drawers that can be pulled out for examination. The cabinet is a contemporary version of early cabinets that were built to preserve ancient curiosities.

A simple timber-framed cabinet constructed without a back creates a hanging doll's house for this collection of figures and furniture. The simplicity of the design is reminiscent of Shaker-styled furniture and is similar to rustic Georgian cabinets. Old cases such as a pie safe or printer's chest, aged or painted with faux marbres, *make charming settings for toy collections.*

Sixteenth-century collectors were past masters at transforming their collections into breathtaking and awe-inspiring spectacles. This twentieth-century glass-and-steel cabinet follows suit. The magnificent structure rises through five storeys parallel with the staircase that extends the full height of the house. Gaps in the structure allow access to rooms. The extraordinary collection of large fairground figures would make an impressive display in any setting, but here the colourful community floats along the corridors of the light-filled cage as though they were alive.

Whether it's a collection of Han dynasty Chinese ceramics, or turn-of-the-century crackle-glaze vases by Sir Edmund Elton, an uncomplicated and elegant elmwood French provincial cabinet (c.1850) will protect such a precious collection and display its beauty admirably. Unlike ornate seventeenth-century cabinets, these alternatives can be found moderately priced at country house sales.

This extraordinary eighteenth-century mahogany cabinet teems with innumerable curiosities, from the smallest pieces of Roman and Greek sculpture to the largest of unlikely objects of naturalia. This triangular example is an exception to the standard rectangular cabinets of the same period that were made to hold casts of engraved sealstones or coins.

drawers. Princely collections, however, were housed in cabinets embellished with precious jewels, silver and engraved ivory. Exotic woods, particularly ebony, were the most fashionable choices for the cabinets produced at Augsburg and Nuremberg in the mid-sixteenth century. Skilled woodworkers became known as 'cabinetmakers' and their virtuosity was measured by their ability to produce these elaborate pieces of furniture.

In the early part of the seventeenth century, Antwerp was known for its cabinetmaking. Designs were mainly chest-shaped, but by the middle of the century larger cabinets supported on legs were being made in a combination of tortoiseshell and ebony for a striking effect. These

cabinets rivalled those produced by the Dutch makers, who decorated their furniture with elaborate floral marquetry in exotic woods, as well as those made by the Italians with *pietra dura* panels, such as the Badminton Cabinet made for the 3rd Duke of Beaufort.

European cabinetmakers flooded into Britain following the restoration of Charles II, and produced cabinets with marquetry incorporating olive wood or kingwood. Japanned cabinets decorated with chinoiserie scenes and rococo gilt brass handles became popular from the end of the seventeenth century, while eighteenth-century pieces favoured the Chinese preference for ornamentation with pagodas. Tastes shifted once again later in the century,

A grand Dutch buffet from the eighteenth century makes an elegant display case for a dinner service of rare Loosdrecht porcelain in Duivenvoorde Castle, near Leiden. The warm rich plum-coloured interior and gilded highlights set up a contrast against the cool green exterior to create a suitably serene setting for fine-quality porcelain.

Plain white or decorated china looks sumptuous against a contrasting colour such as the bright pumpkin orange interior of this dresser. The blue-green exterior balances perfectly with the tones of the shelves, without overpowering of the collection. Experimenting with colour is always worthwhile to achieve the most harmonious backdrop for a display.

when cabinets, many of them designed by Robert Adam, featured tapered columns and pilasters, echoing the architecture of the room.

British makers including William Burgess, Philip Webb and Charles Rennie Mackintosh produced cabinets of great distinction and originality in the nineteenth century, and by the early twentieth century, Vienna was the centre of development for dramatically new cabinet styles, created by designers such as Koloman Moser and Josef Hoffman. Today, although the elaborate cabinets from the sixteenth and seventeenth centuries fetch high prices, collectors can opt for nineteenth-century imitations or obtain reasonably priced antique ones. Japanese staircase

chests or even Chinese teak clothing chests make imaginative alternatives. You can even commission a one-off design from a contemporary cabinetmaker. A less expensive option would be to scour flea markets and antique shops for old shop cabinets, such as those from haberdashers which have glass doors and endless drawers.

Regardless of its design or size, a cabinet is a hiding place for precious things. For the collector of small antiquities, such as gold weights, coins, medals, spoons or seals, the pleasure of reaching inside a drawer and unwrapping an object from its worn paper is all part of the appeal. For many, the secrecy and inaccessibility involved can be intoxicating.

Shelves

A vast array of materials can be used to produce shelves of all shapes and sizes. Apart from perennially popular wood, contemporary shelves are constructed from toughened glass, plastic-coated metal and sheet steel, to name but a few of the technologically advanced materials used today. Modern designs break with traditional straight lines; zigzag patterns and curves are just as practical and far more striking. Whatever your choice, bear in mind that good shelving should be inconspicuous: a poor system will stand out as an eyesore and ruin a display.

Shelves come in two basic forms: freestanding or built-in. One of the prime considerations for some collectors when they are buying a new house is that there should be enough shelving to accommodate their entire collection with room for its ongoing growth. Freestanding units work well in this situation because not only can they be dismantled and transported elsewhere, but they are also designed to grow with a collection: additional units can be added on. Modern universal shelving systems, complete with aluminium tension poles, can be attached to the wall, or compressed between the floor and ceiling, making a useful partition or screen. In period homes where it would be difficult to fix shelving to ancient wood panelling or delicate plaster, a freestanding system would be ideal.

Despite the lack of these benefits, fitted wooden shelves are aesthetically pleasing to the eye, particularly those made from fine wood using traditional cabinetmaking techniques. Their architectural designs and stature make them unrivalled pieces of furniture in their own right and excellent display surfaces for all sorts of collections. Built-in shelves can be made in a range of woods, such as classic mahogany or beech or more affordable woods, such as pine. These can be left plain and untreated, finished with varnish to create an antique effect, or painted any shade to complement the surrounding decor.

A range of decorative finishes can be used to create an atmosphere or continue the theme of a room. Edging the shelves with gilded leather, for instance, creates a formal atmosphere reminiscent of an eighteenth-century library, while decorative mouldings or hand-painted decoration adds an individual personal touch. Lining the back wall with mirrors, or the whole inner surface with patterned wallpapers adds depth and focus.

Above: *Neutral in colour and uncomplicated in design, these simple wrought-iron and brass baker's shelves almost disappear against the bright greens and yellows and abstract patterns of the ceramics they support. The rough hand-painted appearance of this spongeware and yellow-ware pottery would be spoiled by a colourful or decorative unit. Like a drying rack, the wire grilles of the shelves allow the dishes to stand upright or sit on their bases for easy access and use. These shelves would look equally at home in a modern high-tech interior or rustic farmhouse kitchen.*

Opposite: *A series of plain cream-coloured consoles provide perfect neutral supports for a fine collection of green, brown, black and Chinese yellow wide-brimmed bowls by the ceramicist Lucie Rie. The staggered heights of the shelves and the mirror glass behind allow the bowls to stand out against the reflected abstract backdrop, and presents an all-round view of each object. The resulting multi-dimensional effect works well within this modern setting.*

For book collections, many bibliophiles recommend using wooden shelves with a rounded edge to protect the spines. For books of different sizes, adjustable shelves are not necessarily the best solution as books of similar size are usually displayed together. If you intend to have shelves tailor-made for your collection, it is best to decide on a module size and have all the shelves made to these dimensions. Tall books can be placed on their sides, while small books can be double-stacked. If you are a true perfectionist, you could copy Samuel Pepys and have individual, leather-trimmed wooden stands made for the misfits so that their tops align perfectly with your other books. A cheaper alternative would be to fill the gaps with items from other collections.

Take care to choose a thickness of shelving that can bear the weight of the collection as well as looking in proportion with the items on display. Thin shelves suitable

Below left: Anything goes when it comes to creating your own quirky style of shelving. Here, a collector has created a humorous freestanding unit using long cylindrical terracotta pots to support thick lengths of painted wood. The neutral colours blend well with the white and beige tones of the collection.

Below right: Suspended by tension-wired cables, sections of glass shelves dispersed across a wall make a decorative, yet unobtrusive display space for ancient terracotta vessels and ceramic plates. Those pots which cannot stand freely are supported by Plexiglas cuffs.

Opposite: A box shelving unit, made up of 16 cubes, creates a cool modern display. This type of unadorned shelving unit is ideal for arranging mixed collections, each cubby hole providing an individual niche for a small group of compatible items. Setting the white shelves against white walls allows the unit to melt into the background and highlights the colours and shapes of the objects on display – a winning scheme for fans of minimalism. Brightly coloured or decorated shelves would create visual tension with such a diverse collection of objects.

for delicate items will need a series of supports spaced at intervals along their span, while thick wooden ones of 25mm/1in will only need supports at intervals of about 90cm/36in, depending on the load.

Sets of shelves work well as a means of both storage and display, particularly when you want to assemble a collection *en masse* in one area of a room. However, if you want to show off each individual object to the full, then a single shelf running beneath a picture rail can be far more effective.

Shelving can be fitted just about anywhere – on or above doors, recessed into their frames, in between windows, fitted on walls in pyramidal configurations, or bent into sculptural shapes. Playful and humorous or strictly formal, the style you choose will be successful if you select materials and shapes to suit your collection. For example, heavy shelves of oak or slate supported on columns harmonize well with earthenware pottery. Glass shelves are generally used to support delicate glass or china objects; however you can set these on individual carved wall brackets or on consoles arranged in a symmetrical, staggered or pyramidal style. Chinese *famille-rose* porcelain will sit resplendently on rococo giltwood consoles; contemporary Venetian glass vases look good on uncomplicated, semi-circular clear glass bracket shelves; and model sailing yachts suit simple plain wooden ledges.

Raw materials for shelving can be equally as imaginative. Decorating and hardware shops supply shelves made in marble, slate, chipboard, pine, or MDF (medium density fibreboard); they can be painted, covered in fabric, or left as they are. You can vary the look further by your choice of supports: wooden balls held together with steel rods, twisted spindles or hand-forged steel brackets – the choice is endless. Anyone with a collector's eye for style and proportion can fashion their own peerless forms.

Shelves consisting of small alcoves, whether plain wood or gilt, lend themselves to the display of tiny objects. When using confinements of this size, the decisive factor is scale. Objects that are too large will dwarf their space and appear clumsy; too small, and they will look insignificant. You can, however, group very small items together to fill extra space where necessary.

Vases in clear and brightly coloured glass provide a dazzling display. Rather than outshine the objects, the mirror glass doubles the impact of their sparkling translucence. The reflective surface adds light, depth and the illusion of space in a room where such a large-scale collection might otherwise be overwhelming. A regular feature in homes of the 1950s and '60s, this type of display unit is now regaining popularity, particularly amongst collectors of glass and ceramics of these periods.

Lighting

Lighting is the most important aspect of display. With the right amount of light from a chosen direction, even the most modest object comes to life. We experience light on a daily basis, so inevitably we tend to take its power for granted. It is in the absence of light, during dark wintry days, that we most appreciate the profound effect that light has on our moods and feelings. In a gloomy atmosphere our spirits are blighted, but when a blast of light dispels the gloom our mood lifts in an instant.

The intensity of visible light or illuminance relates to the observed brightness of an object; this is the light which is reflected back to the eye. As colours and textures reflect light in different ways, the same amount of illuminance can produce varying results. Rays of light are tools for experimentation. They can be scattered as they pass through a non-opaque substance such as glass and create diffused light, or refracted or bent when passed obliquely from one transparent material into another of different density.

Form, too, is shaped and affected by light. The masters of the Renaissance, such as Caravaggio, produced gradations between light and dark that made flat two-dimensional shapes appear three-dimensional. This modelling with light, known as *chiaroscuro*, influenced many painters of the time. The wonder of light has never ceased to fascinate. The Impressionist Monet painted the façade of Rouen Cathedral more than 20 times, capturing the building from dawn until dusk in all seasons, to show the poetic dimensions of changing light. As he painted, the artist discovered that changing light conditions affect colour as well as shape – an important factor to bear in mind when lighting your own collection.

When light falls on an object, its surface absorbs some colours and reflects back others. Thus, when an object appears green, it has absorbed all colours except green. Our perception of colour – whether light is 'cool' or 'warm' – is expressed in terms of temperature. Yellow and red are warm, while blue and green are cool. Colour rendering is also important, as all too often objects appear to be a certain colour because light is reflected back off their surrounding coloured surfaces. A light source that possesses true colour rendition is often referred to as being colour-balanced and these are the sources of light that are usually preferred by designers and museums.

When lighting a display, the aim should be to reveal the beauty of works of art in an equally elegant way. However, the best methods for doing this are constantly being debated by private collectors, museum staff and conservation experts alike. Paintings, for example, are often illuminated using traditional picture lights in elongated cases. These contain tubular tungsten filament lamps and are usually held on short arms very close to the tops of pictures. Tungsten filaments are biased towards the red end of the spectrum, however, resulting in poor colour rendering. The other drawback with this type of system is that the distribution of light also tends to be inconsistent. Most of the light is concentrated at the top of the picture producing damaging heat and causing the eye to focus on the brightest areas, rather than on the whole image.

Naturally, an effective lighting scheme aims to correct all these failings. Paintings can be lit by special bulbs that have a continuous spectrum designed to resemble sunshine. Set on long arms at some distance from the painting, the lights cast an even illumination over the whole image. Sophisticated fibre optics can also be used to reduce reflections and the build-up of heat when lighting displays in cabinets. Projects of such scale and sophistication are the work of a specialist, but provide inspiration for collectors who are keen to achieve similar results.

Recent advances in lighting technology mean that there is now little excuse for an unsympathetic lighting scheme. If you understand the basic principles of lighting and are willing to experiment with techniques, you will discover for yourself the versatility and power of light. Once you have learned how to make the most of both natural and artificial light, you will be amazed at the range of effects that even the simplest scheme can produce. Seek out professional advice when it comes to the latest developments in fibre optics, lasers, holograms and light-carrying plastic films, by all means, but draw on your imagination first.

Opposite: *Light casts eerie, elongated shadows of spinning whirligigs against a wall. In natural daylight this display appears as a simple playful montage, but at night, at the flick of a switch, artificial light seems to enlarge the painted pine figures and endows them with individual personalities. As the figures mingle and meld with their shadows, the eye is tricked into believing some sort of magic is at play.*

Left: *Throughout the day, the natural light falling on this arrangement acts like a spotlight moving along a set path. Light changes from harsh to diffuse depending on the weather and the time of day, altering the assorted colours in this collection. The main difficulty with natural light is in controlling the amount that falls onto a display. However, for objects that are not harmed by excess levels of light, natural illumination poses no such problem.*

Below: *Placing assorted shapes of candles at different heights produces a romantic still life with a warm glowing atmosphere. Soft lighting like this is perfectly suited to very personal collections such as these seaside treasures. Candle-light produces a sense of occasion and intimacy all at once, but take care to keep naked flames away from anything that is liable to melt or catch fire, and never leave a candle-lit display unattended.*

Right: *Direct artificial light immediately draws the eye towards the objects being lit, creating a striking effect. This form of lighting is a useful device for diverting the viewer's attention away from an unattractive feature in a home or office space. Here, a single tungsten halogen lamp lights up a collection of shells, offering good colour rendering. Directed from one side, the lamp focuses sharply on some surfaces leaving others dim and unlit. Soft, diffused light from an overhead source would be far less dramatic.*

Below: *Artificial light directed upwards onto the white ceiling above this collection provides a uniform controllable source of light that has a rather flattening effect. This method of illumination is useful, however, for evenly distributing light and for avoiding the disturbing glare caused by stray light against glass. Additionally, the damaging ultraviolet component of light will be absorbed if bounced off a high-tinted white surface.*

Below: *Miniature chairs fall under the spotlight creating a sense of theatre. Light reflecting off the mirrored background accentuates the forms of the chairs and simultaneously allows an interesting rear view. The shadows created by this lighting scheme could be minimized by adding light. Alternatively, they could be altered by reflecting light off the ceiling or wall. Notice how different surfaces react to light in opposite ways: light reflects off the metal chair, causing a distinct glare, but is absorbed by the leather seat.*

Above: *Dominant lighting from the upper right emphasizes the shape, form and texture of this contemporary sculpture. This type of lighting is known as 'modelling', and can be either sharp and dramatic or subtle and discreet. Here light bounces off the surface of the sculpture to reveal the object's three-dimensional quality.*

A downward beam of bright light sets this 1960s Murano glass bottle by Zuccheri aglow, emphasizing its elegant form and the quality of its surface. This method of illumination is useful for high-lighting specific features of a glass object with equal emphasis, such as the shoulders, body and base of this bottle. Excellent results can be achieved using fibre optics or low-voltage tungsten halogen spots.

Harsh lighting from one side illuminates a group of terracotta sculptures, highlighting their rough-textured surfaces and throwing interesting shadows on the wall behind, giving them a large looming presence. The interplay of figures and shadows creates a sense of drama and mystery. For a contrasting effect, diffused light could be reflected off the ceiling and back wall to fill in the shadows.

The metal surfaces of this collection of powder compacts gleam under a single source of hard light, emphasizing their textures and minute irregularities. The oblique lighting is directed from a single source, making the left-hand side of the display more prominent than the right. Placing the light further away would reduce its intensity and focus.

Soft light directed from above and reflected off the pale plaster backdrop gives these bold ceramic objects strong definition and distinctly separates them from the background. Highly diffused light shining from the front would flatten their shape and form, but this approach reveals detailed features, such as the mottled surface of the ostrich egg and the sensuous curves of the coupe.

Artificial Light

Advances in technology have produced lighting equipment capable of producing a vast range of effects from the most basic to the most sophisticated. However, simple reflectors and spots are all you need to work your own magic, making it possible to stage interesting illusions and draw attention to features such as unusual textures and shapes.

Artificial sources allow you to display your collection literally in its best light; to direct and control precise lighting situations. Various intensities of light can be achieved to create special effects: ambient light produced by shaded lamps can simulate general daylight, while moving or kinetic light generated by computers can create bright illusions ablaze with colour.

A softer form of artificial light is candlelight, which behaves almost as natural light in the way that it glows, flickers and casts moving shadows. Similarly, its intensity is affected by the surrounding conditions and is capable of creating moods that vary from light and romantic to those of great drama or mystery.

Below left: The strong lines and shapes of these ceramics remain bold and distinct against a dark background even though the acrylic painting and wooden table-top have absorbed a significant amount of the ambient and directed light. The object on the right steals the show in this display as the distinct line between light and shade appears to split its perfect form in half.

Below right: Light shines up through a glass shelf, scattering its rays and casting diffused light over three curvaceous vases. The closer the diffusing material is in relation to its subject, the softer the effect as light reaches the objects from a wider range of directions. Uplighting accentuates the rounded bases of these objects, making their tops appear shadowy in the residual illumination.

Opposite: Hand-made white porcelain ceramics make a striking impression in this cleverly lit setting. The strong directional light defines their hand-cut surfaces, while any shadow is absorbed into the background. The objects appear isolated from their background, almost suspended in space: the effect, loaded with suspense and intrigue, is one that is often used in museums.

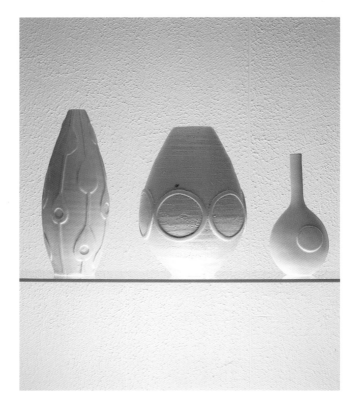

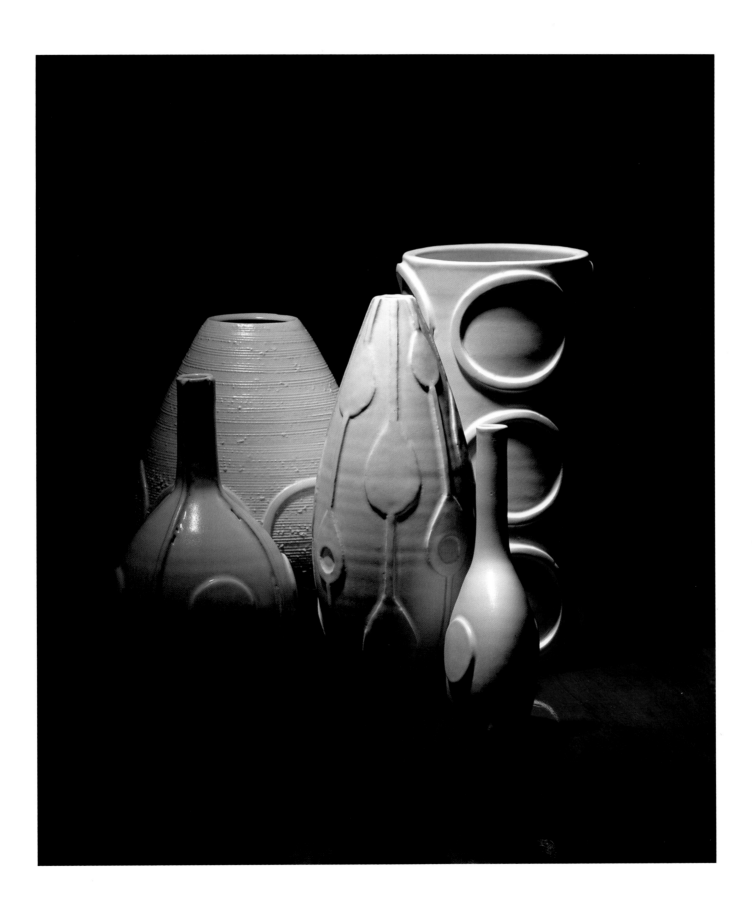

Left: *Ambient natural daylight is generally soft and highly diffused. Accordingly, it creates minimal visual impact, particularly on white objects against a white background, as here. Although the pattern and surface detail of the ceramics are still clear, their depth and dimensions are flattened by this form of lighting. Provided enough light is present, perceived colours appear constant. If the background wall was painted a strong colour, the colour rendition of these objects would be distorted.*

Below: *Diffused backlighting and ambient light gently bathe this collection of ceramics, casting faint shadows in the foreground. Under a single direct source of light from the back, the objects would appear as solid shapes in silhouette against the window. Stained glass and translucent screens, such as fine textiles, respond well to backlighting, from either a natural or artificial source.*

Natural Light

Many collectors prefer to use natural daylight to illuminate their collections. As the day draws on and seasons change, the quality of light alters, changing the whole mood of a display. Daylight is not limited to a colourless stream of brightness; there is scope for innovative effects such as installing panels of coloured glass in windows or doors, for example, to produce a rainbow of brilliance.

There are two basic types of natural light: ambient light which is a general overall diffused light, such as sunlight on an overcast day, and direct light, which is undiffused and comes from one point through a window or skylight. While sources of natural daylight cannot be controlled, their effects can be manipulated with the use of blinds, shades, tinted glass, translucent screens, filters or reflectors. All of these props help to control illumination, particularly where protection from damaging light is needed. Just as importantly, they help to create displays that are as unpredictable as natural light itself.

Direct sunlight from an oblique angle bleaches out the relief detail on part of a group of ceramics, casting faint shadows over the rest. To emphasize textures, turn lights and objects through 360 degrees until the most effective illumination is achieved. A single source of hard light tends to overdramatize texture and produce featureless black holes, although sometimes with interesting abstract results.

Conservation and Security

NO MATTER HOW LARGE OR SMALL your collection of artworks, proper care is essential to preserve it for future generations. It is impossible to include details on every type of conservation treatment, but in the following pages we have set out some basic advice on handling, cleaning and storing artworks. In addition, the appendix lists a selection of books that contain more detailed information on the needs of your collection and how to care for individual items. The more you know about your collection, the easier it will be to choose a reliable conservator or restorer.

First you must decide what you would like to have done to the object in your possession. Does it just need to be cleaned and properly stored, or is it in need of repair and restoration? In some cases this work does not require specialist skills and you may be able to carry it out yourself; more complicated procedures, such as the repair of missing sections or certain methods of cleaning, should only be attempted by trained hands.

In most countries, conservation professionals have considerable practical experience as well as the theoretical and scientific knowledge to help them assess the condition of your object; make suggestions as to the best way to conserve it and retard further deterioration; as well as advise on the optimum methods of storage and display. Most conservation professionals have been trained on an accredited conservation course, usually at graduate level or above, or have served many years as apprentices, learning their craft from experienced conservators at museums or libraries. Unfortunately, as the profession is generally unregulated by law, some of those who advertise themselves as conservators or restorers are self-taught, and their techniques may not be the most appropriate for your object. Reliable conservators can sometimes be located through your local museum or a historic preservation trust, but it is worth consulting one of the national conservation organizations for advice (see page 181 for addresses).

Opposite: Establishing a system of record-keeping for collections is essential. Each item, or part of an item, should be recorded, and dimensions, present condition and any previous conservation treatments noted. Large collections will also benefit from being numbered. On some objects, this can be done by choosing an obscure spot, brushing on a barrier layer of clear varnish and then painting on the registration number using acrylic paint.

The terms restorer and conservator are often used interchangeably, yet the function of each of these professionals is very different. Whereas a conservator arrests the damage and decay affecting an object and then carries out preventative treatment to make it stable, a restorer undertakes procedures that aim to return the object to its original appearance. Restoration can play a part in the conservation process, but conservation is concerned with the total care of your object.

Conservators will be able to advise you on the structural stability of an object and can also determine whether chemical or physical deterioration is taking place. Glass, for instance, is very vulnerable to changes in relative humidity, and glass that was manufactured between the seventeenth and nineteenth centuries, in particular, can deteriorate rapidly once chemical changes within its microscopic structure have started to take place.

The best conservators are often in great demand, but when you do find someone you trust, the first step is to commission a full examination of the object. The conservator will provide you with a written report proposing the most suitable course of treatment, based on the aesthetic and historical significance of the item as well as how you plan to use or display it. For example, if a carpet is to be used rather than displayed, the conservation treatment needs to be tailored accordingly. The potential limitations of any treatment should also be pointed out. Before signing a contract, always ask how long the treatment will take, whether the conservator is covered by insurance and if there will be any additional charges, such as shipping or materials. Some conservation procedures can be very time-consuming and expensive, and treatments may not increase the item's value.

When the work has been completed, you should receive a treatment report (often including photographs of the work in progress) listing the procedures performed and the materials used, along with recommendations for care, display and storage in the future. It is essential to keep the report for future reference: the object may need further care, and, in some cases, treatments might need to be reversed. This sometimes happens when the materials used to restore the object have themselves deteriorated: on porcelain, for example, the yellowing of certain finishes is often something that needs to be dealt with at a later stage. Future generations within the family may also wish to insure or sell the object; knowing how and where it has been repaired is an essential part of its history.

Works of art may not last for ever, but by following basic, preventative conservation guidelines when displaying and storing collections, the level and rate of deterioration can be minimized. Recommendations for light, relative humidity and temperature levels have been included in the entries that follow, along with suggested methods for controlling air pollutants and pests.

Monitoring environmentally induced damaging factors assists in their control. Lux meters are easy to use and even the inexpensive models will provide adequate readings of the intensity of visible light, measured in units of lux. Ultraviolet (UV) light, in the invisible part of the spectrum, is measured with a UV monitor. As these are expensive, it is best to ask a conservator to take the necessary readings. As temperature affects relative humidity (RH) as well, these two are often measured together on thermohygrographs. Many inexpensive models are inaccurate and as the instrument needs to be placed in proximity to the collection, you may need to consult a specialist.

Paper is so commonplace in most people's lives that few stop and think about its humble origin over 2,000 years ago. Discovered by the Chinese, it was originally made from scrap cuttings of cloth that were beaten, mixed with water and poured over a bamboo screen. Once dried, the matted sheet was paper. The secret of its manufacture gradually spread to the West, and by the twelfth or thirteenth centuries paper was being produced in Italy and Spain. The pure composition of paper was gradually adulterated: first by the addition of size (a glue-like substance) and, in the seventeenth century, by the addition of chemicals such as alum to increase acidity, and thus strength and durability. In the late eighteenth century chlorine was used in paper-making. Many of these additions actually cause paper to darken and lose its strength, speeding up the deterioration of works of art on paper.

As demand for paper increased, a substitute for cloth had to be found, and in the mid-1800s the first groundwood pulp mill was built in the United States. Wood-based papers deteriorate much faster than those made from cloth, which is why today, such ephemeral items as news-papers are printed on these less permanent materials. Traditional hand-made papers are still available: the most durable ranges are manufactured from an acid- and alum-free slurry made of the purest fibres of cotton and pure high-alpha cellulose. Some of these have alkali added to act as a buffer against the acid contamination that results from handling.

Environmental conditions

If you want to preserve your work of art on paper, whether it is a print, water-colour, collage, drawing, map, stamp, poster or photograph, it is essential to keep it in the correct environment. Moulds grow in excess humidity and heat, while light and pollution are also contributory factors in the deterioration of paper.

Ideal conditions for paper items are those in which the temperature and humidity remain constant. This limits the degree to which the paper expands and contracts, both aspects that can cause structural damage. It is difficult to meet these criteria in most homes, but you should aim for a temperature of 5–21°C/60–70°F with a relative humidity (RH) of 55 per cent. Temperature can easily be controlled with central heating and air-conditioning systems, but maintaining correct humidity is harder. Portable dehumidifiers can be used and lowering the heat will also help.

Avoid storing or displaying works of art in poorly ventilated bathrooms and basements where fluctuations in temperature and humidity can be extreme. Mould, small brown spots (a mould growth in the paper itself is called foxing), rusting hanging wire and flaking paint are all signs of excessive humidity levels. The best way to tackle the problem is to unframe or unmount the work of art and allow it to air. Flaking surfaces will need the immediate attention of a conservator.

Light is the external factor which is most detrimental to works on paper. Light damage is cumulative and irreversible and leads to changes in appearance and structural deterioration. Natural daylight contains ultraviolet (UV) rays which are the most destructive. Fluorescent and tungsten halogen lighting contain high proportions of UV, too. Incandescent (tungsten) light bulbs produce less UV, but they do emit damaging heat. A maximum of 50 lux is the recommended intensity of light for paper objects. To reduce UV levels in display areas, use curtains or blinds, and fit lights with incandescent bulbs. Many museums use UV-filters and cover fluorescent tubes with plastic filtration sleeves. UV-filtering acrylic or glass can be used in frames or windows to the same effect, but because of their potentially damaging static charge, acrylics should never be used next to pastels or charcoal.

The clusters of rusty, brownish coloured spots obscuring this print, known as 'foxing', are caused by a type of mould that flourishes in acidic papers kept in conditions of high relative humidity (above 65 per cent). The item should be unframed and allowed to air dry, before being remounted in acid-free board and displayed in an area where the relative humidity is less than 55 per cent.

In an ideal world, no print, drawing, map or any work of art on paper would ever be exhibited, but as this is generally unrealistic, you can compromise by limiting the amount of time anything is on display. Most museums rotate their works, adopting a three-month cycle of exposure per year for each artwork. Damage by fading may seem minimal, but by the time you notice it, it is already too late to repair.

Pollutants are readily absorbed by porous paper, leather, parchment and vellum. Sulphur dioxide, a major constituent of smog, is one of the most harmful contaminants. Once absorbed, it is converted to acid, causing discoloration, brittleness and the disintegration of the fabric of most items. In polluted environments, the best strategy is to limit the introduction of outside air. Unfortunately, the filters on most residential air-conditioning systems cannot reduce outdoor gaseous pollutants.

Indoor pollutants, such as tobacco smoke and the fumes from oil-burning furnaces and cooking, can be minimized with good ventilation or simply by displaying your collections away from these irritants. Alternatively, you can use archival mounting boards which contain substances designed to trap certain pollutants.

Insects love the gelatine sizing in paper and the glue used for mounting. Monitor your collections carefully, looking out for insect remains or damage, and keep the area as clean as possible. Sticky traps will provide you with better evidence of what pest is causing the damage. If you do find evidence of insect damage, place the work of art in an airtight plastic bag and contact a conservator for help. Eliminating pests is very difficult and should be undertaken only by a professional exterminator; insect sprays and most fumigants are harmful and should be avoided.

A prime food source for insects and vermin, books can quickly be reduced to an outline of their former selves. Damp, warm environments encourage infestation. This item is beyond repair, but others in the collection may be saved if a conservator is asked to advise on the best conditions to display them.

Most insecticides are chemical based, but non-toxic methods of treating infestations in all organic materials, including wood, paper, textiles, leather, books, frames, documents and entire rooms or buildings, are also available. A technique developed in Germany known as Thermo Lignum uses warm, humid pressurized air in a chamber over a period of 12–24 hours to treat objects. The high temperature (55°C/130°F) kills the eggs, larvae, pupae and adults of the major pests. Results are encouraging, and it is hoped that this technique will help to phase out toxic insecticides currently being used.

Handling and care

As well as being vulnerable to damage by poor environmental conditions and insects, paper items are all too easily damaged by careless handling. With just a little care and common sense, you can avoid unwittingly inflicting damage on your own collection.

• Ensure that your hands are clean before handling items such as books and drawings. If possible, wear white cotton gloves, as oils and acids from your hands are easily transferred to paper.

• Hold items with both hands to prevent bending, creasing or tearing, and never put unmounted works directly on top of each other; separate them using uncrinkled, acid-free tissue.

• Some works of art are easily scratched, so be careful not to touch or drag anything across the surface. Never use any kind of adhesive tape, glue, or heat-sealing mounting tissue.

• Mount all valuable items between acid-free boards. If this is not feasible, keep them in acid-free folders, or in envelopes stored in acid-free boxes, drawers or museum storage boxes (made from acid-free board). Wooden drawers should be sealed with a water-based polyurethane coating and lined with a barrier material such as Mylar, because wood emits acidic gases. Anodized aluminium or steel drawer units can also be used.

• Even mounted material should be protected with acid-free tissue when on display, and all mounts should be opened from the outer edge to avoid depositing acids and oils inside.

• Never roll paper items. Place them flat between stout boards before transporting.

Mounting and framing

Works of art should never be placed directly against glass, as the condensation produced encourages mould. There is also a risk of the picture sticking to the glass. A mount not only protects the item, it allows it space to move beneath the glass as atmospheric conditions change. Mounting also prevents the yellowing of images. Any reputable framing store will do this for you but it is not difficult to do yourself. You will need a mount knife for cutting the window, an all-rag mounting board, a buffered rag board, and 'conservation' or 'museum' board, which has a neutral pH. The recommended thickness is 4-ply for general use and 8-ply for pastels, collages and large pictures.

The basic window mount is simply two pieces of board hinged together with a strip of gummed cloth tape. The lower margin of the board should be slightly larger than the upper. Leave a space about 3cm/1¼in all around the image to prevent it from being damaged when the mount is opened and closed. Using the mount knife, cut a bevelled edge around the opening and lightly sand down the sharp edges. Hold the item in place by attaching it to the backboard with hinges made from high-quality gummed paper, or Japanese paper, and fixed to the upper edge of the back side of the piece using starch paste. Depending on the size and weight of the item, cut two strips at least 1cm/½in wide and fold them in half before applying them first to the picture and then to the backboard. Cover the boards with blotting paper before leaving the mounted piece for a few hours under a light weight to dry.

To protect the item from dust, dirt and insects, add a protective layer of sturdy, lignin-free cardboard at the back of the frame. Hold it in place with nails, or metal or wooden braces secured with screws. Finally, seal the gap between the backboard and the frame with gummed wrapping tape, which does not render it airtight but allows the frame to breathe.

PHOTOGRAPHS

To increase your understanding of the best means of caring for your photographs, it is essential that you first identify the processes that have produced your image. The various types: daguerreotypes, ambrotypes, tintypes, silver, platinum and cyanotypes, all have their own specific preservation requirements. Basically, a photograph is made up of a base support – paper, metal or glass – followed by a binder layer, which contains the light-sensitive salt that forms the final image. All photographic processes are inherently unstable and, as with all works of art on paper, photographs require specific environmental conditions and careful handling. There are many excellent books on the subject of identifying your photographic images.

Most of the common problems associated with photographic images, such as torn, cracked, or soiled images, require a photographic conservator. Never use cleaners on images, as this will only result in loss. If an image is stuck to glass or you have broken glass negatives or ambrotypes, place pieces carefully in archival-quality paper boxes or envelopes and seek the advice of a specialist conservator.

Environmental conditions

All photographic materials need cool, dry, well-ventilated conditions. As with other works of art on paper, increased humidity will encourage mould and mildew, breaking down the fabric of the image. Generally, a temperature of 20°C/68°F with a relative humidity of 30–40 per cent comprise ideal conditions, although contemporary colour photographs prefer lower temperatures of about -4°C/30–40°F. Subsequently, many museums now have cold-storage areas to house their collections of colour photographs.

Like other works on paper, photographs are easily damaged by light and pollutants such as sulphur dioxide, so it is

Accurate identification of photographic processes and the causes of deterioration are essential before conservation treatments can begin. The loss of emulsion on this print is probably due to the breakdown of the transparent binder layer caused by fluctuating temperatures and humidity.

important to limit the amount of time they are on display and to control the amount of light: 50 lux should be the maximum.

Framing and mounting

Photographs are best protected by being framed (see page 164). If you cannot frame your whole collection, however, protect your photographs by keeping them in stable plastic or paper folders that are free of acids, sulphur and peroxides. Photographs, unlike other paper items, should be stored in unbuffered paper because the alkaline buffering that is added to some archival storage papers can alter the photographic image. Although daguerreotypes and ambrotypes usually have their original cases or frames, an additional custom-made paper enclosure will help keep them in good shape. Uncoated polyester film, uncoated cellulose triacetate, polyethylene and polypropylene (certain slide pages are made of this and should be used) are suitable materials for plastic enclosures. All of these are chemically stable. A word of caution here, however: high humidity (above 80 per cent) will cause emulsions

to stick to the surface of plastic, so these should not be used in such extremes. Avoid using plastic with glass-plate, nitrate, or acetate-based negatives, too. Other materials to keep away from photographs include brown paper envelopes, polyvinyl chloride (PVC), rubber bands, paperclips, tape and rubber cement. Archival-quality albums can be used to display family photographs. Avoid self-adhesive and magnetic albums and those with highly coloured paper.

Handling and care

Most damage to photographs comes from bad handling, so many of the guidelines for handling works of art on paper apply (see page 164). In addition:

- The surfaces of photographs are easily and indelibly marked by fingerprints, so it is best to wear cotton gloves.

- Use a camelhair brush or photographer's blower brush to remove dust.

- Avoid using ink pens around photos; pencils used lightly on the reverse will cause the least damage.

PAINTINGS

Whether you are a collector of paintings or not, you will be familiar with the inevitable symptoms of ageing: a darkened or yellowed surface caused by the years of grime, or discoloured varnish; cracks on the painted surface; flaking paint; mould; and even tearing. In some cases where, for example, there is an increase in the transparency of oil paint, there is nothing that can be done to stop these processes from taking their course.

Paintings consist of a number of layers. The support can be made from a variety of materials: wood (called the panel, often with additional wooden battens to prevent warping), fabric (which will have a wooden frame or stretcher to help it keep its shape), leather, glass, plaster, or ivory. The majority of paintings have either a fabric or wooden support, and this layer is usually primed with size or another ground material, but many examples of folk art and some contemporary paintings are unprimed. The paint layers can be made up of pigments in acrylic, oil, wax (encaustic), egg (tempera), or gouache (plant gum), and are often finished with a coat of varnish. Proper framing is best undertaken by reliable professional framers. Local galleries or museums can often recommend someone in your area.

Environmental conditions

The complex layering of the various parts of a painting means that it is essential to keep relative humidity and temperature constant. High humidity causes the rather flexible canvas to become slack. If this happens, the much less flexible layers of paint can crack and in some cases loosen and fall away. The best conditions for paintings are the same as those for people: a relative humidity of around 40–60 per cent and a temperature of 20°C/68°F.

Paintings are easily damaged by light, particularly direct sunlight, which causes fading and a deterioration in both varnishes and paints. Direct heat should also be avoided. Hanging a picture above the fireplace might seem an ideal location, but soot, heat and extremes of conditions will do it no good. Equally, siting pictures above heating and air-conditioning vents or in a poorly ventilated bathroom is inadvisable. To minimize damage, position paintings in indirect light or use UV filters on windows and light fittings. The infra-red portion of light is especially damaging because the heat energy it emits is absorbed by the painted surface, causing chemical deterioration. Use IR-reflecting solar glasses and films to reduce solar heat gain through glass.

Lights attached to, or hanging directly over, pictures can be dangerous. Instead, set them at a sufficient distance to minimize the transfer of heat to the painting. The eye responds badly to contrast so take advantage of the fact and hang dark paintings against dark walls. As a result, lower levels of illumination will be needed for the viewer to see the picture comfortably. The recommended museum standard for lighting oil paintings is 150–200 lux. Light damage is cumulative and therefore rotating the display of your collections is a sensible measure.

Handling and care

Handling your pictures can be hazardous and it is important to take as much care as you can. Attaching a protective backboard made from Foam-Cor (archival cardboard backing) will help slow the progress of any possible environmental changes to the support, assist in keeping out dust and dirt, and keep the painting safe while it is being handled. Refer to the following guidelines before attempting to move your paintings:

Paintings age at various rates causing colours to darken or lighten, become yellow or fade away. In the right-hand picture, accumulations of dust and varnish have been successfully removed by a trained conservator, a process which needs to be undertaken with caution to avoid harming the original paint surface.

• Very large paintings or those with unusual frames may require professional handlers. Remember that it will cost more to repair a damaged picture than to employ the services of experienced professionals.

• Determine first whether you are able to lift and carry your painting safely. In general, if the frame is wider than your shoulders it is not wise to attempt to move it on your own.

• Before lifting a painting, move any furniture, carpets or pets that are in your pathway and prepare a space in advance to put it down.

• Always use both hands when lifting a painting. With the painted side facing you, place one hand on one side of the picture and use the other to support the bottom.

• Before re-hanging the picture, examine the back of the frame to make sure the fittings are secure, with no loose rings or worn wires. Always hang pictures from hooks rather than nails; large works will need two hooks. The wire should always be attached, in double strands, to rings or plate hangers that have first been secured firmly in the wooden frame.

• If paintings are to be hung on outside walls, attach rubber spacers to the back of the frame to increase air circulation.

Examine your pictures every six months or so for loose paint and insect infestation in the frame. Any major structural damage, such as flaking paint, cracks or tears, will need to be treated by a trained picture restorer. Yellowed varnishes should also be removed by a specialist. To dust, use soft natural fibre brushes made out of badger or sable hair – but watch out for loose paint. Never use cleaning solutions, feather dusters, insecticides or furniture polishes near pictures.

The problems and goals for the preservation of furniture and musical instruments are very similar. Both are often composite objects, which means they are made up of both organic materials (from animal or vegetable sources) and inorganic materials (such as metal and glass). The conservation requirements of each of these substances is different. An additional factor to consider is that both items are functional: furniture is made to be used and instruments to be played. Creating and maintaining a suitable environment is therefore especially important in protecting these objects and prolonging their life.

Environmental conditions

As we have seen, light can have dramatic effects on the objects, particularly those made from wood and organic materials. It is not always practicable as it is with some other works of art, to rotate the display of furniture because of its size and constant use. As wood is especially vulnerable to bleaching by exposure to strong light, it is particularly important to protect wooden pieces from direct sunlight using blinds, shutters or curtains. Where possible, darken rooms in which they are displayed.

Temperature and humidity levels should be kept between 18–24°C/65–75°F and 55 per cent relative humidity (plus or minus 5 per cent). Once again, it is best to maintain stable conditions where possible. Both instruments and furniture expand and contract with fluctuations and extremes of temperature and humidity – veneered furniture and inlaid instruments are susceptible to such changes.

Insects flourish in moist conditions and especially love wood. Infestation can spread rapidly throughout a whole collection of furniture, including your piano, so keep an eye out for powder on the floor (called frass), as this means there is activity. Seek the advice of a conservator to help eradicate the pests.

Handling and care

Proper care must always be taken when moving furniture to avoid damage. Always use reputable movers and ensure that the item is well wrapped. Crating furniture for shipping is best left to experts, but do make sure that they take into consideration the need to create a microclimate (an artificial environment that controls heat and humidity) for certain valuable objects if they are being moved to a new environment with different conditions.

• Use webbing to handle heavy objects – wherever possible, separating furniture into its component parts before moving.

• Remove any shelves and tie down or lock doors to prevent them opening.

• If the object is particularly heavy or awkward, ensure that enough people are available to carry it.

• When carrying musical instruments, always be careful to well clear of any sharp objects. If the instrument is likely to come apart, pick it up cautiously using both hands. Wear cotton gloves when handling brass wind instruments.

Lifting veneer, missing corners or legs, ink stains, chipped gilding, loose joints, and so on, are all jobs for a professional furniture restorer. Joints, hinges and blocks need to be maintained and loose fittings mended by a professional. Seat surfaces, such as cane, often need to be repaired. Upholstered seats all have special needs, depending on the covering fabric, and should be vacuumed with a net covering on the nozzle of the cleaner in order to prevent damage to their surfaces and to make it easier to retrieve any loose trimmings that may be pulled off.

Handling and cleaning gilded or lacquered furniture needs particular care, Most can be dusted lightly with a soft cloth, but painted or inlaid furniture should be cleaned only with a sable brush.

Furniture constructed from a combination of different materials – for example, various woods, silver, bone or ivory inlays, and gesso with metal gilding or paint and lacquers – poses a real challenge for a conservator as such items often demand a variety of treatments. As furniture is generally functional, the main aim will be to restore its original appearance and working state.

It is best to avoid using water-based cleaning solutions on wood; if your furniture has a layer of grime, remove it using a slightly dampened soft cloth, but only having tested a small section first to make sure the water does not cause it to change colour. Never leave a damp cloth on a wooden object for any length of time; the rings left by the moisture from glasses are a reminder of how easily it can be damaged.

High-gloss French-polished furniture needs only a hard rub with a clean, soft cloth – only professional polishers should attempt to smooth out any imperfections. Waxed furniture requires more care and, in addition to weekly dustings, beeswax should be applied three or four times a year. To do this, first apply a small amount of mineral spirits to a clean cloth to moisten it, then take some wax and work it into the surface using a circular motion. Leave it to be absorbed by the wood for several hours before buffing to a shine.

The requirements for care of a historical collection of musical instruments may depend on whether you are hoping to play your collection or to display it – some collectors do both. Playing an old wooden instrument which has not been played for years often causes it to crack because of the sudden introduction of moisture. If you must play it, break it in gradually and clean it out after each use with an absorbent cloth brush specially made for this purpose. Metal instruments may have been coated with lacquer which has now yellowed, so you may need to consult a trained conservator if you want to remove it. Keyboard instruments are often inlaid, veneered or painted, and in these cases, all the conservation needs must be satisfied by specialists. Stringed instruments are very susceptible to humidity changes, and warping is a common problem when the instrument has a wooden frame. Only clean and polish your instruments when absolutely necessary, using a soft, dry cloth to wipe off any dust.

TEXTILES

This category encompasses an enormous variety of objects: costume, lace, hats, shoes, beadwork, fans, samplers, curtains, carpets, tents and dolls. These are often composite objects, consisting of either natural or synthetic fibres along with a host of other materials, such as metals (beads for instance), horn (a natural plastic often found in fans) or even glass (buttons). This makes many of the techniques of restoration quite complicated and demanding. Whether they are quilts used to cover the beds of our forebears, or fans that have lain hidden for years, all textiles need to be displayed in conditions that will help them to survive for the enjoyment of future generations.

Environmental conditions

Light is the chief enemy of textiles because in fading and damaging the fibres, it causes them to become weak and brittle. As with works of art on paper, you can minimize exposure of your piece to direct light by rotating your collections and filtering any light source you use. Ideally, use a lux meter to ensure that the light intensity is no higher than around 50 lux.

High humidity is harmful to textiles, as it encourages the growth of mould, causes colours to bleed and attracts insects. Air pollution too, especially sulphur dioxide, is damaging to metal beads and threads. As almost everyone has experienced when they have taken their much-loved jumper out after the summer, insects love textiles, both to feed on and lay their eggs in. The Thermo Lignum technique (see page 164), which rids your works of art of insects at all the different stages of their life cycles, has proved to be particularly effective on costumes and textiles of all kinds.

Handling and storage

Even if your textiles are not on display, incorrect storage can cause as much damage as careless handling.

- Line drawers with acid-free tissue or board.

- Never fold textiles. The creases will not only leave unsightly folds but will also cause cracking. Either lay them flat, interleaved with acid-free tissue, or roll them onto an archival rolling tube, or calico or muslin fabric, finishing with a layer of undyed muslin. Not even large textiles should be folded. Roll them onto an acid-free tube interleaved with acid-free tissue and cover the complete roll when finished.

- Costumes, both historic and contemporary, can be stored flat in an archival box or hung (if condition allows) on hangers wrapped in layers of polyester quilting to pad the support. Cover with undyed muslin. Modern costumes, which often have plastic components, should never be stored with other items, as plastics frequently emit harmful by-products as they degrade.

- Never use polythene as a cover. Dust covers should be made of undyed cotton muslin and need to be big enough to protect the whole costume.

- Hats are easily crushed in storage and should never be left resting on their brims. Keep them in acid-free boxes, resting on cushioning rolls of acid-free tissue to preserve their shape. Special stands, made for museum storage, can also be obtained.

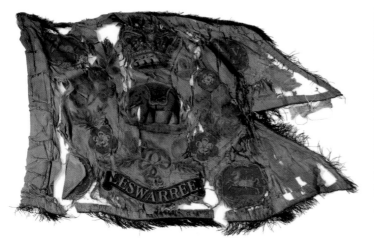 

Textiles are extremely sensitive to the entire light spectrum, but professional conservators can take even the most damaged of objects, like this 1801 silk guidon, and return them to their former glory. The delicate painted silk, coupled with the heavy decorative fringe, demand that special care is taken when the item is displayed.

- Fans, too, need to be cosseted either in acid-free tissue or kept folded and placed in their original boxes, which have been lined with acid-free tissue.

The repair of all large textiles, from carpets and rugs, to tapestries and tents, is best left to experts, as their sheer size makes it almost impossible to undertake even simple tasks. Basic cleaning can, however, be carried out on all but the most fragile textiles. Carpets that are walked on daily will obviously need more frequent vacuuming than those that are hung on walls for show. Do remember to vacuum the back of the item too, as dirt and dust gets trapped between the knots and can be hard to remove. Fragile textiles should be vacuumed at a low power and through a nylon mesh – in order to catch any loose fibres. Always avoid using rotating brushes when cleaning textiles. Many conservators recommend sewing a strip of cotton tape to the ends and edges of carpets to give them additional support and prevent damage. Any structural damage, such as stains or fraying edges and tears, must be handled by professionals.

There are several acceptable methods of mounting textiles for display. Sturdy textiles, such as quilts or tapestries, can be hung using Velcro. Stitch the fuzzy side of the Velcro to a cotton webbing strip the length of the top edge of the textile. Hand-sew the strip on to the item and staple the hook side of the Velcro to a varnished batten of wood. Attach the batten to the wall and press the two tapes together. Textiles requiring more support can be sewn on to fabric-covered archival board, or for larger items, on to mounting fabric stretched over a wooden frame. Use only 100 per cent cotton fabrics that have been prewashed to remove dyes and sizings. The stitching should not pull the fabric or allow it to sag; add a few stitches in the centre if needed. Mounted items can be framed, but if so, do not allow the glazing material to touch the textile.

DOLLS

Like so many of the objects discussed so far, dolls are made from a range of materials, including wax, wood, bisque, papier mâché, china, textile and celluloid. Each component requires specific care and conservation treatments, but there are certain hazards that are common to them all.

Environmental conditions

Minimize exposure to strong light, especially daylight, using the methods outlined on page 169. Light will fade the colour of the dolls' clothes and their hair.

The paintwork on faces of bisque and china dolls can change colour within months of exposure to strong daylight, while celluloid dolls will become bleached and brittle. Strong light produces heat which harms all materials, especially wax. The wax may not melt, but light will cause the pigment in the wax to fade. More dramatically, many a wax doll has been destroyed when placed too near an open fire. Dolls' glass eyes – often secured with wax to allow them to open and shut slowly – can also be affected by warm conditions. All dolls benefit from being kept in relatively cool conditions.

Water is often seen as a harmless cleaning agent, unfortunately, it is lethal to bisque dolls, whose eyes are suspended on a trapeze-shaped device held in place by two blobs of plaster of Paris. If water gets into the eye socket, it weakens the plaster, causing the mechanism which opens and shuts the doll's eyes to come unstuck.

Handling and care

Although most dolls were originally made to be played with, great care should be taken when handling and displaying them. Dolls are frequently exhibited in a seated position; but this is usually very unstable and is the cause of many cracked and even smashed heads. Use nylon fishing line to attach the doll firmly to a padded cushion and prevent needless damage.

SOFT TOYS

Stuffed soft toys seem to suffer most from the ravages of dogs. The children who love and play with them are also the cause of all kinds of wear and tear: arms are left hanging as they are twisted in their sockets, eyes are pulled out and general limpness sets in as the toy's stuffing is pulverized to dust. There are numerous specialist restorers who can help put life back into your collection, but it cannot be stressed enough that you should never be too drastic with your repairs. As with many objects, the value of soft toys often decreases as a result of over-zealous restoration. If in doubt, always seek the advice of an expert.

Environmental conditions

Like all textiles, soft toys are easily damaged by direct light, so keep light levels to a minimum for valuable objects to prevent discoloration and embrittlement of the textile fibres. Aim for a light intensity of around 50 lux. Try to keep soft toys away from moisture, as this encourages insects, mould and bacteria growths, which are common causes of damage. If they do become infested, seal them in a polythene bag with moth balls. Alternatively, for prized soft toys infested with insects, the Thermo Lignum technique (see page 164) is recommended because it is a toxin-free procedure.

Handling and care

Remove dust from soft toys using a long-nosed vacuum with nylon netting fitted over the nozzle. If more thorough cleaning is required, gently sponge the surface with a gentle baby shampoo or non-ionic detergent applied with undyed paper towels or a soft sponge, being careful to use as little water as possible. Leave to air dry. Never immerse stuffed toys in water or place them in a tumble dryer.

METAL OBJECTS

Metals are made by taking various ores, melting them together and then shaping them, using a combination of methods. We may think that metal objects will last forever, regardless of their condition, but this is far from true. Over time, and depending on their environment, metals tend to convert back to their natural ore state through the processes of corrosion, or oxidation. The purest metals, such as gold, are less prone to this process.

Environmental conditions

As with all works of art, relative humidity, temperature and pollution all need to be regulated in order to provide the best conditions for metal objects. Corrosion, which causes the most damage to metal, takes place in the presence of moisture. It is therefore advisable to try to keep your relative humidity as low as possible: 40–45 per cent is a good level for which to aim. Controlling this by means of temperature is not advised and should only be undertaken with caution. A sudden drop in temperature in an enclosed space will cause condensation on the surface of metal objects.

Plastics, fabrics, woods and adhesives all produce corrosive gases that can damage metal objects. Lead toy soldiers are especially vulnerable, with damage appearing as a white powdery residue known as lead disease. The source of the problem often has its origins in the animal glues used to assemble the original wooden storage cases, as these were often stabilized with acetic acid. To find the source of the corrosion, place a piece of scrap lead in the area where you would like to display your objects. If the lead develops spots or a whitish tinge, one or more of the substances in that area is producing organic acids which will attack the metal.

Handling and care

All metal objects, whether they are gold, silver or lead, need careful handling. Museums now require all staff to wear cotton gloves when working with objects.

- Take care to avoid letting metal objects rub or hit other objects. Scratches (especially to softer metals) and dents are an all-too-familiar sight.

- Lift objects using both hands, and when possible, carry them in padded baskets or trays.

- Use acid-free tissue and polyethylene foam sheeting as cushioning and for wrapping objects for storage. Avoid using plastics: some give off gases that will form harmful acids, while others deteriorate and stick to the surface.

Although gold in its pure state does not corrode, it is rarely made into objects without being alloyed either with silver or with copper, both of which corrode. Ancient gold, silver and bronze artefacts can be brittle and are often covered with corrosion. Such a layer should never be touched except by experts, as removal could damage the underlying metal surface, destroying clues to important information at the same time: how the object was used in ancient times, for example.

Remove surface dirt and dust from uncorroded objects with a soft brush, cotton swabs dipped in ethyl alcohol, or a puffer brush. Surface tarnishing on silver can be removed by using commercially available removers but avoid those containing tarnish inhibitors and silver-dip solutions, and ensure that any non-silver areas, such as inlays, are covered with plastic wrap to prevent any adverse reaction. If silver has been deliberately darkened by its maker, it should be left unpolished.

Over time, polishing gradually removes the silver metal. To prevent silver from tarnishing, use paper or cloth storage bags containing activated carbon. Many museums apply a protective coating of reversible resin or lacquer, but these can yellow, and should only be used on objects that will be displayed.

Excessive polishing of silver can wear away engraved decoration along with the metal itself. Storing and displaying silver with anti-tarnish papers, or cloths containing activated charcoal, allows the gases that cause the blackening to be absorbed, preventing the need for frequent cleaning.

STONE OBJECTS

Copper alloys, which include bronze (copper and tin), brass (copper and zinc), and even copper on its own (small traces of other minerals are always present), are easily corroded by chlorides and sulphide gases. A light green powdery corrosion on the surface of copper alloy objects is a common sight, especially on ancient objects recovered from the soil. This type of corrosion is known as bronze disease and, if it is left untreated or if the object remains in an environment where there is high humidity, the process will continue unheeded. Always consult a conservator for advice on treatment.

Never use any of the recipes for cleaning bronze and brass that can be found in many household cleaning manuals because these may strip off finishes or patinas and thus devalue the object. It is often hard to ascertain whether what is on the surface is part of the object or not, so when in doubt, contact a trained person. Often bronzes were painted or waxed, and this layer should never be removed. As with silver, lacquer can be applied to protect the surface. This procedure is highly recommended for sculpture that will be kept out of doors, otherwise the elements will certainly destroy any patina added by the foundry. Maintenance on these outdoor works of art is high: they need to be inspected regularly in order to catch any breaks in the coating which might trap moisture and aid corrosion. Existing corrosion should be assessed by a conservator.

Certain metal objects, such as ancient coins, may need unusually low humidity levels to prevent deterioration. The recommended relative humidity of below 35 per cent can be achieved by placing pre-conditioned silica gels such as Art-sorb or ARTEN Silica Gel into a closed display or storage case, creating a specialized micro-environment. A humidity-indicating strip placed inside the case will show when the silica gel needs re-conditioning.

Some of the earliest man-made objects, such as axe-heads, arrows and scrapers, were made from stone. Like metal, stone is often considered a permanent material. Unfortunately, if the object is positioned out of doors, exposed to the elements, acid rain will rapidly dissolve the carbonaceous and siliceous components of marble, limestone and other stone. In addition, extremes of temperature, salts, mosses and other growths will also encourage decay.

Environmental conditions

Unlike most of the objects we have mentioned, stone tolerates quite a range of temperature and relative humidity. However, where possible, extremes should always be avoided. For example, very high humidity encourages biological growths. Many archaeological stone objects will present an added complication: salts may have seeped into their fabric. Fluctuations in relative humidity will cause these to crystallize, damaging both the surface and internal structure of the object. The first indication that salts are present is a powdery surface, and in this case it is very important to maintain a relative humidity of around 50 per cent.

Handling and care

Stone objects are able to soak up oils from your hand, and many soft stones like alabaster can be easily scratched. Follow the advice given for handling metal objects (see page 171). Most stone objects can be cleaned using a vacuum with a soft bristle attachment. It is very tempting to clean darkened marble sculptures, but this is best left to a trained conservator. Over-enthusiastic cleaning can obliterate detail on marble and other stone objects, and is generally to be avoided.

The porosity of this stone Buddha makes it susceptible to unsightly stains from a number of causes, the most common of which are the leaching out of natural iron (iron pyrites) from the stone when saturated with moisture, biological activity and atmospheric pollution.

CERAMICS

There are many different types of ceramics, ranging from bone china to low-fired earthenware. They are usually grouped by their porosity and firing temperatures. Restoration and conservation procedures vary for each group, but the basic care of all ceramic materials is the same.

Environmental conditions

With ceramics, unlike other materials, it is not light, temperature and humidity that are the main concerns. They invariably suffer most as a result of poor handling, display and storage. Nonetheless, extremes and sudden changes of temperature should always be avoided, as this may cause cracks and damage to glazes. High light levels are harmful because of the rapid temperature changes they produce. While for most ceramics, humidity does not lead to problems, mould growth does occasionally occur, and can cause staining unless it is removed.

Low-fired ceramic ware can also suffer from salt damage, which is usually related to its past environment – for example, objects recovered from the sea or used as storage vessels for pickles or other foods. This problem is often manifested as a white efflorescence on the surface, and may cause spalling of the surface layers. Salts can be removed by soaking the object in regularly changed baths of tap water, but it is best to keep such objects in conditions with a low relative humidity.

Handling and care

Basic common sense will ensure proper handling of this material.

- Never hold objects at their weak points, such as the handle, spout or top edges, and always use both hands.

- Never stack ceramics. Before transporting ceramics, remove lids and pad generously, using conservation-quality packing materials.

Glazed earthenware pots are vulnerable to contamination by water-soluble salts which penetrate any unglazed areas. At low relative humidity, these salts will crystallize, forcing the glaze to break off.

- Never apply self-adhesive stickers to the surface of ceramics, as these can leave stains and lift off glazes when removed.

Loose dirt and dust can be removed with soft, clean white cloths or soft brushes, but avoid using chemical cleaning sprays. If dirt persists, try to remove it with a dampened cloth. As long as they are in good condition, most ceramics can be washed using a non-ionic detergent in a sink lined with soft cloths; you should never wash unglazed earthenware, however, or any ceramics that have been repaired, painted or contaminated with salts. Staining on ceramics, in particular bone china, can result from everyday use. Tea, coffee, grease, even shellac and epoxy used for repairs can penetrate all types of ceramics, but if the glaze on a porous item is cracked or damaged, these can seep under the glaze and into the fabric. If the item is not irreplaceable or highly decorated, try soaking it in a warm, dilute solution of biological washing powder (avoid doing this with low-fired ceramics). A conservator may use either baths or poultices of dilute alkaline solutions with organic solvents to encourage the stain to move; alternatively, hydrogen peroxide may be used to alter its colour and make it less obvious.

If breakages occur, save the pieces, wrapping them individually in tissue to avoid wearing away their broken edges, and take them to a professional for mending.

GLASS

Glass has been used for nearly 4,500 years, initially to make beads and amulets, and later to make a wide range of objects, from drinking vessels and lamps, to windows, mirrors and even writing implements. It is an artificial substance made from the fusion of a silica, such as sand, quartz or flint, with an alkali like soda or potash. Other substances are sometimes incorporated: lime for durability and lead oxide to add weight and brilliance. In Ancient Egypt glass objects were cast, cut from blocks or fashioned on a clay or mud core. Later manufacturing methods included glass-blowing and mould-pressing.

Environmental conditions

Most glass will not be adversely affected by its environment; direct sunlight, however, should be avoided. High relative humidity can cause unstable glass (glass that is high in soda or lead) to weep, or to produce moisture on the surface. If subsequently exposed to low relative humidity over an extended period, the glass will slowly dry out. The breakdown of the structure leads to the appearance of fine cracks, commonly referred to as crizzling. A stable environment of around 40 per cent relative humidity should be maintained to prevent further deterioration.

Handling and care

At the risk of stating the obvious, glass requires the utmost care when handling. It is only too easy to knock over glass objects, and thin clear glass is particularly difficult to see.

• Never handle a glass item by its weakest point, such as a spout or handle; instead use two hands, with one supporting the main body of the object at all times.

• Avoid handling glass objects in the middle of the afternoon when one tends to be most weary. This is when most breakages occur.

• Use a padded container if the object needs to be moved a great distance.

Superficial dust can be removed by using a soft paintbrush or soft cloth, but avoid commercial cleaners. Most antique glass objects can be washed in water, except for those where there is crizzling, iridescence (flaking), decoration or a repair. Line your sink with soft cloths to prevent chipping, then use a mild solution of non-ionic detergent in warm water to wash, taking care to avoid applying pressure on the glass while cleaning. Drain and follow up by gently polishing with a soft cloth.

Chipped or cracked glass requires special adhesives and repairs are best left to a conservator. Residues of flaked glass, limescale, wine or perfume will need to be cleaned by a glass restorer. Mirrors that are flaking or have worn surfaces can either be re-silvered or have their appearance improved by the insertion of a reflective surface behind the missing areas. Glass in windows has to contend with the elements: acid rain attacks the structure of glass as well as the lead and putty holding the pieces together. Where the glass is friable, or the lead weak and brittle, a conservator must be called in to make the necessary repairs.

Many glass objects are difficult to restore because of 'springing', the release of internal stress in the material caused by some manufacturing processes. As a result, repairs will never be perfect: cracks and breaks may be misaligned, and adhesives applied often remain visible.

Many of the pigments used on ethnographic objects are natural, light-reactive paints, so they are likely to fade if displayed in unfiltered light with a high ultraviolet component.

ETHNOGRAPHIC COLLECTIONS

Unlike many of the objects discussed, the value of ethnographic items is greatly increased if information about their place of origin is preserved along with the object. For this reason, these items should be cleaned with special care to ensure that any traces of substances such as resin, oil, tar and wax are left intact, as these may reveal critical information about the item's usage and place of origin. The composition of ethnographic collections can be organic (made from plant or animal materials) or inorganic (made from materials such as stone or metal) or a combination of both.

Environmental conditions

The diversity of ethnographic collections means that there is often a conflict between the optimum conditions for the various different types of materials. As a general rule, it is best to avoid great fluctuations of temperature and relative humidity. Avoid placing items in areas near a source of heat and keep light to a minimum (around 50 lux), using UV filters where possible, as natural materials

will fade and degrade. Recommended temperatures are between 15–22°C/59–71°F – generally the cooler the better – and organic-based collections prefer a relative humidity of 50 per cent. Pollutants and dust can cause damage, but insects are probably a greater problem, so watch out for frass and cocoons. If you do find evidence of an infestation, isolate the object immediately and seek professional advice.

Storage

Where possible, use archival-based products for storage. Custom-made supports can be constructed using polyethylene foam, cut to shape and lined with acid-free paper, but avoid any chloride-derived materials or those containing plastics. Pad out objects to prevent creases using cotton wool rolled up in acid-free paper, and cover with polyethylene sheeting or undyed muslin to protect them from dust. High-quality metal cabinets are best for storage. Inspect your collection regularly, as early detection of unexpected hazards is the best form of protection.

TAXIDERMIC AND NATURAL HISTORY COLLECTIONS

Shells, insects, plant remains and mounted vertebrates, all require specific methods of cleaning, conservation and storage. There is little written about the care of these types of collections; all major natural history museums have experts, however, who should be willing to advise on specific needs.

Environmental conditions

As for ethnographic materials, extremes of light and humidity, insects, fungal growths and pollutants will all increase the rate of deterioration of your collections. Animal-based proteins, such as skin, feather, bone and fur, respond readily to changes in humidity and temperature, quickly causing specimens to distort and decay. Light is detrimental to animal-based materials and continued exposure causes fading, especially if the item has been coloured with natural dyes. Plant and fibre specimens require conditions similar to those described for paper objects (see pages 162–4), and they easily become brittle and so prone to structural damage.

Insects love natural materials; moths in particular are known for their ability to destroy wool, feathers and fur. Keep a look out for signs of infestation and act quickly if any is found. Caution must be taken when handling older taxidermic and organic-based objects, as many of the older methods of insect-proofing used arsenical preparations and mercuric chloride powder: white powder or crystals will alert you to the use of arsenic products, while black or darkening spots may indicate mercury compounds. Use disposable gloves to handle these and keep them away from pets and children.

Handling and mounting

Insects should be mounted using stainless-steel pins. Steel or brass pins corrode and can cause damage so these should always be replaced with stainless steel.

Cork was traditionally used as a base to stick the pins into; nowadays, Plastazote or similar synthetic materials covered with acid-free paper are recommended. Small shells should be stored and displayed in glass tubes with acid-free cotton wool or cellulose wadding. Larger items can be kept in boxes made from acid-free corrugated board that has been buffered with 3 per cent calcium carbonate to guard against acids. Be careful to avoid storing or displaying shells in unsealed wooden cases, because a white efflorescence will form on the surface as acids are gradually released.

Many mounted vertebrates are protected by being displayed inside a case. Larger specimens are generally too cumbersome to be displayed in this way, however, making them especially vulnerable to damage. In particular, leg wires, originally used for additional support, often need to be replaced. Great care is needed when moving mounted vertebrates, as their bases are often too insubstantial to support their weight. In addition, the glass tops of cases are often not secured to the base. It is tempting to refurbish case-mounted birds and mammals; one can touch up the background if needed.

Replacing missing tails, ears and feathers, however, should be left to the experts. Keep cleaning to a minimum, wiping with water-based solutions and using brushes to rid the object of moulds once these have been killed. Mounted specimens of bone should be handled with gloves to avoid contamination with skin oils, and a sable brush is recommended for dusting these objects. If your collection is large enough, a compressed air blower with a trigger-action nozzle will be invaluable for cleaning. Minor repairs can be carried out using pottery-mending adhesives, such as epoxy and acrylic resins.

This bird of paradise has been saved just in time from the ravishes of moths. Infested objects should be removed immediately from display, isolated in a sealed bag and treated, before being re-exhibited. Any other items in a collection, particularly those made from animal proteins, should also be checked for signs of attack.

FOSSILS AND MINERALS

Fossils can be found in a number of substrata, including clay, shale, limestone, sandstone, coal, marl and amber, to name but a few. Fossils found in these various substances require specific methods of extraction and conservation, and since there are so many different types, and as any treatment or care is dependent on the condition of the individual fossil, it is best to seek the expertise of a professional from a local museum or geological association. However, there are some basic guidelines that apply to the care of all such collections.

Environmental conditions

Although rocks, fossils and minerals seem, by their very nature, to be indestructible, good care and storage is essential for their long-term survival. The most satisfactory temperature for these artefacts is around 15°C/59°F, plus or minus a few degrees. Humidity can be harmful, causing chemical changes, especially with pyrite. Pyrite rot causes yellow and white efflorescence, cracking the specimen as it oxidizes, and changing it from iron sulphide to ferrous sulphate and sulphur dioxides. These specimens should be kept in conditions of low humidity – around 30 per cent. Little can be done if pyrite decay has already begun. A trained conservator, however, can remove and neutralize the products of acid oxidation.

Many fossil books recommend applying a coat of lacquer to protect the surface; some even suggest soaking specimens in a lacquer solution. In the past many types of coatings were used, including shellac, Bakelite and polyvinyl acetate, but none of these is impermeable to air or moisture, so they will not prevent oxidation.

Absorbed water should be removed from pyritic fossils by placing them in a desiccator. They should then be stored in airtight polythene boxes with desiccated silica gel to absorb any further moisture.

Even seemingly indestructible objects, such as this ammonite preserved in pyrite, require careful handling to avoid damage. Inexpensive display cases and carrying cases are easily custom-made using plastic or cardboard boxes lined with acid-free paper, and fitted with a piece of inert foam that has been cut with a hole just large enough to hold the fossil snugly.

,Other kinds of fossil materials, such as shale, ivory and sub-fossil bone, should be kept in conditions of high relative humidity, about 50 per cent, as low humidity causes these moisture-absorbent specimens to shrink. Store this type of specimen in airtight boxes with silica gel preconditioned to the appropriate relative humidity of approximately 50 per cent. Some minerals can change colour when exposed to harsh light, so very sensitive specimens need to be kept in the darkest possible conditions.

Handling and care

Wet cleaning can be done on most specimens using organic solvents or water with a non-ionic detergent (although you should avoid cleaning anything with pyrite in it). To clean fossils with water, roll moistened cotton buds across the surface, and then blot dry with absorbent paper. Dry cleaning, too, can be undertaken using a soft brush, rubber granules (draught clean) and a vacuum. Many old

collections of fossils were stored in wooden display cabinets; these should always be sealed with two coats of polyurethane varnish, or replaced with those made from powder coated steel. All specimens should be kept in acid-free tissue and supported with polyethylene foams, which are chemically inert.

Labelling is essential, as information about where and when a specimen was found is a major part of its value. Water-, insect- and tear-proof labels are obtainable, but the amateur collector might prefer to apply a little lacquer or enamel paint, writing the details onto this using black waterproof ink. Some collectors may like to varnish their specimens to enhance their appearance and protect them. Use a high-quality, high-grade nitrocellulose lacquer (wood-refinishing grade), thinned with acetone or lacquer, and apply this using a hand-held, pump-spray bottle. Alternatively, one could also resort to the acrylic sprays used for fixing watercolours sold in art stores.

PLASTICS

Phone cards, furniture, handbags, jewellery, household goods, radios, televisions and beads are just a few of the many objects made from this complex and fascinating material.

Plastics are all based on long chains of molecules, mainly of carbon atoms but there are many different types. Some are completely natural, such as horn, shellac, rubber and gutta percha; others are based on natural materials that have been chemically modified, such as Celluloid, cellulose acetate and casein. Still others are completely synthetic, such as Bakelite, polyvinyl chloride, perspex (polymethyl methacrylate), polyethylene and nylon. Such variety, along with the addition of fillers, colorants and stabilizers, makes identification of these materials difficult.

The method and date of manufacture, appearance, colour, texture, smell and hardness are all clues to identifying specific types of plastic. For example, Celluloid gives off a smell of camphor when rubbed gently or washed in warm water. Books on plastics and identification kits containing samples of common plastics are available and these will help you to identify the specific types of plastic in your collection.

Environmental conditions

Many people think of plastics as being relatively indestructible. However, although plastics do not rust or tarnish, they will degrade as a result of slow chemical reactions taking place between the plastic material and its environment. Plastics are inherently unstable and demand a very high level of preventive conservation. Light will cause damage to all plastics, such as brittleness and changes in colour, so levels should be kept as low as possible. Try to keep relative humidity stable too, but bear in mind that whereas cellulose materials

need an environment with low moisture, nylon will be harmed unless relative humidity is kept at approximately 60 per cent. Temperatures also need to be kept stable; if the temperature rises above 20°C/68°F, some plastics will melt or deform. Many synthetic and semi-synthetic plastics give off acidic gases that are indicative of their own self-destruction, and will cause harm to nearby materials, like metal, so it is advisable to keep these away from other objects.

Handling and care

Cleaning should be kept to a minimum. Remove surface dust using a dry brush or cloth. If further cleaning is needed, wash with warm water containing non-ionic detergent. There is no need to rub hard; gentle wiping with a soft cloth is best. Use a soft brush to get into crevices. This should be followed by a rinse in clean water and then the object should be dried with an absorbent cloth.

Solvents are best avoided and any object that shows signs of deterioration, such as cracks or crazing, should be kept away from water. Objects marked by tape or other sticky substances may be cleaned with a cloth moistened with a little white spirit or isopropyl alcohol. Test a small hidden area of the object first, and do not rub too hard or allow the spirit to remain on the surface for too long. Ensure that you are working in well-ventilated surroundings when using solvents.

Cellulose nitrate objects were made in the 1920s, under the trademark Celluloid, to imitate ivory, bone and tortoiseshell combs, brushes and accessories. Decomposing cellulose nitrate objects emit by-products that are acidic, corrosive and very flammable. They can neither be restored, nor can this 'cancerous' process be reversed or halted, so collections of plastics demand careful display methods to avoid their demise.

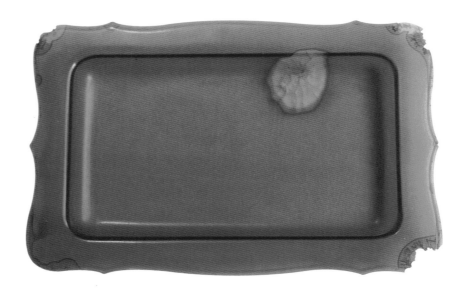

SECURITY

Theft continues to be a major source of anxiety for museums and private collectors alike. Despite the introduction of powerful low-light colour cameras, highly sensitive intrusion detection devices, wireless motion detectors and infra-red curtains, it seems that no matter how sophisticated your system, the criminals can find equally high-tech methods to rob you. On a more encouraging note, the general consensus from those in the business of tracking down stolen art items is that the most effective deterrents are not necessarily the most expensive.

Grilles on windows, iron shutters on doors and large security cameras can make your home seem more like a prison than a place to live and enjoy your collections. However, there are a number of alternative measures that you can take to help deter potential intruders: good outdoor lighting, gravelled driveways, using central timer switches to turn lights on and off at intervals, and good locks on perimeter gates are all effective and relatively low-cost deterrents. In addition, where possible, plant and maintain a thick growth of hedging: berberis, an evergreen shrub with very sharp spines, often known as barberry or nature's own barbed-wire, is highly recommended. Its long spikes will do untold damage to even the most cautious burglar.

If you do feel compelled to install intruder alarms, closed-circuit television (CCTV) or any other high-tech security system, obtain a list of approved security companies from a national security approval council first or seek advice from your insurers. Marking systems can be useful, and several have been developed, including some that use small electronic tagging devices. Unfortunately, the signals from these systems can be difficult for the police to decode and trace. However, another system has recently been introduced that uses forensic science as its deterrent. SmartWater IndSol Tracer is a harmless solution that can be applied to almost anything, from the bases of ceramics and the frames of paintings to garden furniture. Once dry, it leaves a permanent, invisible, chemically coded 'fingerprint' that can be detected by police under ultraviolet light. An international database records each SmartWater-protected item and this can be accessed by law-enforcement agencies worldwide. In addition, like neighbourhood watch schemes, SmartWater warning stickers in windows may deter burglars.

Whether you decide to invest in high-tech security measures or not, everyone should keep good written and photographic records of any valuables. An international standard for describing works of art known as the Object ID Checklist has been drawn up by 84 countries under the umbrella of the Getty Information Institute in Los Angeles. This is used by agencies worldwide, including New Scotland Yard, the British Museum, the Art Loss Register, UNESCO and the FBI in the fight to stem the trade in stolen works of art.

The importance of taking good photographs of your valuables, either yourself or using a professional fine-art photographer, cannot be overstressed. If your objects are stolen, good photographs and documentation will be critical in helping to identify your possessions. If you decide to do your own photography, follow these tips:

• Fill the frame when taking the photograph, taking the shot as close as possible to include maximum detail.

• For a very small object, such as a ring, use a macro lens on your camera and take the photograph using a tripod to avoid a blurred image caused by camera shake.

• Take close-ups of any markings or damage on the object.

• Light objects well, but try to do so without creating shadows. Ambient light in a shady area outdoors is preferable to bright sunshine. Indoor lighting is also good but more difficult to set up.

• Always use a background that will not appear in the image, for example, black velvet is good for all but dark objects, but avoid using the auto-exposure on your camera as it will try to average the tone. Instead, let the meter read the light levels coming off the object itself.

• Finally, include a scale in the picture, either a ruler or, clearer still, a black-and-white scale drawn onto card.

If you feel daunted by taking your own photographs, there are several alternatives. One is to contact the offices of associations of fine-art photographers for a list of security-registered professional photo-graphers. The UK association includes members who work throughout Europe. Another alternative is to contact one of several high-tech companies who are using digital imaging technology: the images will not fade and can easily be stored securely. Some companies can produce a detailed catalogue of each piece, including all the details now required by the Object ID Checklist. Insurance companies usually offer discounts on their policies for those using such services.

Once you have a good photograph and record of your object, the art crime databases in both Europe and America will be able to assist the police in locating your work of art if it is stolen. The Art Loss Register and the Thesaurus Group both have offices in New York and London, and both hold images and details of stolen works of art on a database. The Thesaurus Group, the world's largest processor of auction house information, teamed up with *Trace* magazine to create an Art Crime Tracing System (ACTS) to add to the magazine's hard-copy publication. This provides insurance companies with a very useful pool of information that no police force to date has managed to amass.

CONSERVATION ORGANIZATIONS

Many of the following organizations represent professional conservators and restorers in private and institutional practice. They may be able to refer you to a conservation professional in your area.

The American Institute for Conservation of Historic and Artistic Works
1717 K Street, NW Suite 301
Washington DC 20006, USA
tel: (202) 452 9545
fax: (202) 452 9328
e-mail: vnyaic@aol.com

Australian Institute for Conservation of Cultural Material Inc.
PO Box 1638
Canberra ACT 2601, Australia
tel: (61) 2434 531
fax: (61) 2417 998
e-mail: gina.drummond@
awm.gov.au
website: http://www.vicnet.au/
-conserv/hp.hc.htm

Canadian Association of Professional Conservators
c/o Gerald Fitzgerald
Canadian Museum of Nature
PO Box 3443, Station D
Ottawa K1P 6P4, Canada
tel: (613) 566 4770
fax: (613) 990 8818
e-mail: gfitz@mus-nature@ca

The Conservation Unit
Museums & Galleries Commission
16 Queen Anne's Gate
London SW1H 9AA, England
tel: (0171) 233 3683
*Operates a database listing
conservators and their specialist
areas. For a small fee the unit
can provide contact details on up
to five relevant conservators.*

European Confederation of Conservator–Restorers' Organizations
Secretariat, Diepestraat 18
B-3061 Leefdaal, Belgium
tel/fax: (2) 767 9780
*Can supply a list of many European
member organizations which are
institutes for conservation and
restoration.*

Institut fur Erhaltung von Archive und Biblitheksgut
Attn: Dr. Haberditzl
Schillerplatz 7
D-71638 Ludwigsburg
Germany

Institut Français de Restauration
I–20 DAW
Des Oeuvres d'Art Bibliotheque
150 avenue de President Wilson
93120 La Plaine St Denis, France
tel: (1) 49 46 57 00

Instituut Voor Conservatie en Restauratie
Zwartezusterstraat 34
B-9000 Gent, Flanders, Belgium
tel: (9) 225 4290

The Institute of Paper Conservation
Leigh Lodge, Leigh
Worcestershire WR6 5LB
England
tel: (01886) 832323
fax: (01886) 833688

International Association of Paper Historians
Wehrdaer Strasse 135
35041 Marburg, Germany
tel: (6421) 81758
fax: (6421) 82506

International Federation of Library Associations and Institutions
PO Box 95312
2509 CH The Hague, Netherlands
tel: (70) 31 40 884
fax: (70) 38 34 827
e-mail: ifla.hq@ ifla.nl
website: http://www.nlc-bnc.ca/ifla/

International Centre for the Study of the Preservation and the Restoration of Cultural Property (ICCROM)
via di San Michele 13
00153 Rome, Italy
tel: (6) 585 531
fax: (6) 5855 3349
e-mail: iccrom@ iccrom.org

International Council of Museums (ICOM)
Committee for Conservation
Université Libre de Bruxelles
Faculté de Philosophie et Lettres
CP 175
50 avenue Franklin Roosevelt
B-1050 Brussels, Belgium
tel: (2) 650 24 66/650 24 19
fax: (2) 650 43 49
e-mail: jgallard@resulb.ulb.ac.be

International Council on Archives (ICA)
Ch Kecskemeti, Secretary General
60 rue des Francs-Bourgeois
75003 Paris, France
tel: (1) 40 27 63 06
fax: (1) 42 72 20 65
e-mail: 100640.54@
compuserve.com

International Institute for Conservation of Historic & Artistic Works
6 Buckingham Street
London WC2N 6BA, England
tel: (0171) 839 5975
fax: (0171) 976 1564
e-mail: 100731.1565@
compuserve.com

Les Grands Ateliers de France
8 place de la Madeleine
75008 Paris, France
tel: (1) 42 96 12 75
fax: (1) 40 15 98 32
*A select group of artisans who
are re-evaluated every year and
re-elected into this group.*

Scottish Conservation Bureau
Longmore House, Salisbury Place
Edinburgh EH9 1SH, Scotland
tel: (0131) 668 8668
fax: (0131) 668 8669

Scottish Society for Conservation and Restoration
The Glasite Meeting House
33 Barony Street
Edinburgh EH3 6NX, Scotland
tel: (0131) 556 8417
fax: (0131) 557 5977
e-mail: admin@sscr.demon.co.uk

United Kingdom Institute for Conservation (UKIC)
6 Whitehorse Mews
Westminster Bridge Road
London SE1 7QD, England
tel: (0171) 620 3371
fax: (0171) 620 3761
e-mail: ukic@ukic.org.uk

CONSERVATION REFERENCES

Adams, R. ed. *Preservation of Library and Archival Materials: A Manual* (Washington DC: Technical Information Service, American Association of Museums, 1996)

Buys, S. & Oakley, V. *The Conservation and Restoration of Ceramics* (London: Butterworth-Heinemann, 1996)

Coe, B. & Haworth-Booth, M. *A Guide to Early Photographic Processes* (London: Victoria & Albert Musuem, 1983)

Howie, F. M. *The Care and Conservation of Geological Material; Minerals, Rocks, Meteorites and Lunar Finds* (London: Butterworth-Heinemann, 1992)

Landi, S. *Textile Conservator's Manual* (London: Butterworths, 1992)

Morgan, J. *Conservation of Plastics* (London: Museums & Galleries Commission, 16 Queen Anne's Gate, London SW1H 9AA, 1991)

Newton, R. & Davison, S. *Conservation of Glass* (London: Butterworths, 1989)

Sandwith, H. & Stainton, S. *The National Trust Manual of Housekeeping* (London: Penguin Books, 1991)

Simpson, M.T. & Huntley, M. *Sotheby's Caring for Antiques* (London: Conran Octopus, 1996)

Thompson, G. *Museum Environment* (London: Butterworths, 1994)

Walker, A. & Carter, D. eds. *Care and Conservation of Natural History Collections* (London: Butterworth-Heinemann, 1998)

Many of the organizations listed above produce in-house publications which are available to non-members. In addition, The Getty Conservation Institute provides a mail-order service for an extensive range of in-house conservation publications:

Getty Trust Publications Distribution Center
PO Box 49659-DPT GE27
Los Angeles
California 90049-0659

tel: USA or Canada (800) 223 3431 or (310) 440 7333: refer to code GE27 when calling
fax: (818) 779 0051

Another excellent supplier of books to the conservation and museum profession is:
Archetype Books
31–34 Gordon Square
London WC1H OPY, England
tel: (0171) 387 9651
fax: (0171) 388 0283
e-mail: archetype@ netmatters.co.uk

Their US distributer is:
University Museum Publications
tel: (800) 306 1941 toll free in USA and Canada
or (215) 898 4124
fax: (215) 898 0657

CONSERVATORS AND RESTORERS

Most of the conservation organizations listed above can help find a qualified conservator, restorer or conservation centre in your local area; the following list includes some of those who come highly recommended by a number of sources.

Art Conservation & Restoration Conservation Access at the State Library
Macquaire Street, Sydney
NSW 2000, Australia
tel (2) 9273 1676
fax: (2) 9273 1265
e-mail: consacc@ ilanet.slnsw.gov.au
Conservation of works of paper, photographic material and ephemera. 24-hour disaster recovery.

L'Atelier
106 avenue Marguerite-Renaudin
92140 Clamart, France
tel/fax: (5) 46 48 95 91
Museum-quality restoration of old and contemporary posters.

Brian's Bearheart Hospital
76 Shortwood Avenue,
Staines, Middlesex
London TW18 4JL, England
tel: (01784) 451631
Restorer to the Royal collection of soft toys.

Celia Cammarota & Dinah Swayne
45A Montpelier Grove
London NW5 2XG, England
tel: (0171) 267 9909
fax: (0171) 485 2177
Bookbinders.

Frederic Cocault
5 rue Ernest-Lefèvre
750 Paris, France
tel: (1) 40 31 54 23
Restoration of icons.

Conservation Specialists Ltd.
The Workshop
Camelsdale Road, Haslemere
Surrey GU27 3RJ, England
tel: (01428) 661 981
fax: (01428) 661 983
Artefacts in stone, wood and polychrome surfaces.

The Conservation Studio
68 East Street, Thame
Oxfordshire OX9 3JS, England
tel/fax: (0184) 421 4498
Conservation of all types of ceramic and glass objects.

Peter Cousens Pty. Ltd.
93 Lennox Street, Newtown
NSW 2042, Australia
tel/fax: (2) 9550 3809
Conservation of paintings, works on paper, photographs and frames.

Christine Del Re
Del Re Objects Conservation Services
PO Box 1218, Oak Park
IL 60304, USA
tel: (708) 386 9381
fax: (708) 524 1355
Objects and ethnographic items.

Dolly Daffs
3 Bridge Street, Fordingbridge
Hampshire SP6 1AH, England
tel: (01425) 652450
Call proprietor Allan Gordon to discuss needs before sending dolls.

The Fan Museum
12 Crooms Hill
London SE10 8ER, England
tel (0181) 305 1441
fax: (0181) 293 1889
Conservation of fans.

William Forbes
Deeview Studio
Corriemulzie, Braemar
Aberdeenshire AB35 5YB
Scotland
tel: (013397) 41676
Taxidermist.

David Goldstein
22 Grove Street 2F
New York NY 10014, USA
tel: (212) 627 5368
e-mail: xubzulima@aol.com
Archaeological and art objects.

Roy Graf
17 Shelbourne Drive,
Windsor, Berkshire SL4 4A4
England
tel: (01753) 854474
Paper restorer who has worked on the Queen's collection at Windsor.

Rupert Harris
Studio Five
Number One Fawe Street
London E14 6PD, England
tel: (0171) 987 6231
fax: (0171) 987 7994
e-mail: rupert@ harris-met-con.demon.co.uk
Restorer of fine metalwork.

Hatfield's
42 & 42a St Michael's Street
London W2 1QP, England
tel: (0171) 723 8265/6
fax: (0171) 706 4562
Restorer of furniture and works of art.

HCS Conservation Services
PO Box 733, South Melbourne
Victoria 3205, Australia
tel: (3) 9690 1373
All types of conservation.

International Conservation Services P/L
53 Victoria Avenue, Chatswood
NSW 2067, Australia
tel: (2) 9417 3311
fax: (2) 9417 3102
Also at:
102 Morehead Avenue
Normans Park
Queensland 4170, Australia
tel/fax: (7) 3399 7355
Conservation and restoration of furniture and paintings.

Rebecca Johnston
Williamstown Art Conservation
Center, 225 South Street
Williamstown MA 01267, USA
tel: (413) 458 5741
fax: (413) 458 2314
e-mail: rjohnsto@
clark.williams.edu
Books, paper and photographs.

Leather Conservation Centre
34 Guildhall Road
Northampton NN1 1EW, England
tel: (01694) 232723
fax: (01694) 602070

Monique Leroy
58 rue de Londres
75008 Paris, France
tel: (1) 43 87 17 88
Restorer of porcelain.

**Maureen Martin
Creations Past Ltd.**
The Doll's House
Stonehall Common
Worcester WR5 3QQ, England
tel: (01905) 820792
Restorer of stuffed animals.

Christine Palmer
Carvers & Gilders
9 Charterhouse Works
Eltringham Street
London SW18 1TD, England
tel: (0181) 870 7047

Ellen Pearlstein
The Brooklyn Museum
200 Eastern Parkway
Brooklyn NY 11238, USA
tel: (718) 638 5000 (ext. 276)
fax: (718) 638 3731
e-mail: pearlstn@is2.nyu.edu
Objects of all types.

Beverly N. Perkins
Art Conservation of Los Angeles
37224 Huckaby Lane
Murrieta CA 92562, USA
tel: (909) 698 1520
fax: (909) 698 1618
Sculpture and objects of art.

I. & B. Perryman
100 Queen Street,
Woollahra
NSW 2025, Australia
tel/fax: (2) 9327 3910
*Restorer and cleaner of textiles
and rugs.*

Dennis V. Piechota
Object & Textile Conservation
16 Central Street
Arlington MA 02174, USA
tel: (781) 648 3199
e-mail: piechot@world.std.com
Archaeological objects and textiles.

Plowden & Smith Ltd.
190 St Ann's Hill
London SW18 2RT, England
tel: (0181) 874 4005
fax: (0181) 874 7248
Conservation of all objects.

Eric Price
220 3rd Street No. 2, Troy
NY 12180-4463, USA
tel: (518) 273 5773
e-mail: eprice2256@aol.com
Conservation of gilt wood frames.

RB Instruments
6 Dudson Close, Mt Eliza
Victoria 3930, Australia
tel (3) 9787 8428
fax: (3) 9787 8117
Restorer of scientific equipment.

Clare Reynolds
20 Gubyon Avenue
London SE24 ODX, England
tel: (0171) 326 0458
*Conservator of works of art
on paper.*

**The Royal School
of Needlework**
Apartment 12A
Hampton Court Palace
East Molesey
Surrey KT8 9AU, England
tel: (0181) 943 1432
*Restoration of needlework and
embroidery.*

Katherine Singley
PO Box 65358
Baltimore MD 21209, USA
tel: (410) 312 8852
fax: (410) 321 8852
*Ethnographic and archaeological
objects.*

Sandra Smith
Department of Conservation
The British Museum
London WC1B 3DG, England
tel: (0171) 323 8650
fax: (0171) 323 8874
Books, paper and objects.

**Sotheby's Conservation &
Restoration Department**
34–35 New Bond Street
London W1A 2AA, England
tel: (0171) 408 5305
fax: (0171) 355 3670
Fine art and furniture.

**David Stein
& Tony Ameneiro**
32B Bruton Street, East Sydney
NSW 2067, Australia
tel: (2) 9360 2201
fax: (2) 9360 2261
*Conservation of paintings
and works of art on paper.*

**The Textile Conservation
Centre**
Apartment 22
Hampton Court Palace
East Molesey
Surrey KT8 9AU, England
tel: (0181) 977 4943
From September 1999 relocating to:
Park Avenue
Winchester SO23 8DL, England
*Conservation of all types of textiles
including large tapestries.*

Thermo Lignum UK Limited
19 The Grand Union Centre
West Row, Ladbroke Grove
London W10 5AS, England
tel: (0181) 964 3964
fax: (0181) 964 2969
e-mail: 101 563,1474 @

Compuserve.com
*Non-chemical method to aid in the
conservation of objects infested with
insect pests.*

Thermo Lignum
Atelier fuer Restaurierung und
Sanierung, Thermo Lignum
Landhausstrasse 17
69115 Heidelberg, Germany
tel: (6221) 163 466

Thermo Lignum
Ufficio Cantonale Dei Musei
Viale Franscini 30A
6500 Billinzona, Switzerland

Bill Topping
Lambeth Palace Library
London SE1 7JU, England
tel: (0171) 928 6222
Bookbinding.

**Therese Prunet & Nicole
Tournay**
42 rue Mesley
75003 Paris, France
tel: (1) 42 77 80 30
*Painting restorers to the national
museums of France.*

John Walker
64 South Molton Street
London W1Y 1HH, England
tel: (0171) 629 3487
*Watch, clock and jewellery repair
and restoration.*

Richard de Welles
80 Whiting Street, Artamon
NSW 2064, Australia
tel: (2) 9439 9023
*Restorer and conservator of
fine furniture.*

Roy Zeff
Penfriedn (Burlington) Ltd.
34 Burlington Arcade
London W1V 9AD, England
tel: (0171) 499 6337
Restorer of fountain-pens.

CONSERVATION SUPPLIERS

Acecroft Pty. Ltd.
PO Box 900, Mount Waverley
Victoria 3149, Australia
tel: (3) 9543 0174
fax: (3) 9543 4156
*Restoration and maintenance prod-
ucts for metals and wooden surfaces.*

Art Preservation Services
223 East 85th Street, B2
New York, NY 10028, USA
tel: (212) 988 3869
fax: (212) 794 3045

*Products and consultation for
environmental monitoring and
control. Mail-order service
supplying ARTEN Silica Gel
and monitoring equipment.*

Art et Conservation
33 avenue Trudaine
75009 Paris, France
tel: (1) 48 74 95 82
fax: (1) 42 80 35 38
*Products used in restoration
and conservation.*

Art-sorb (Fuji Silysia Chemical)
121 SW Morrison Street, Suite 865
Portland OR 97204, USA
tel: (800) 795 9742
fax: (800) 295 1832
e-mail: fscpdx@SpiritOne.com
*Art-sorb in beads, sheets or cassettes
for moisture control.*

**Charcoal Cloth
(International) Ltd.**
High Tech House, Commerce Way
Arena Business Park

Houghton-le-Spring
Tyne and Wear DH4 5PP, England
tel: (0191) 584 6962
fax: (0191) 584 6793
*Activated charcoal cloth to reduce
tarnishing.*

Conservation by Design Ltd.
Timecare Works, 60 Park Road West
Bedford MK41 7SL, England
tel: (01234) 217258
fax: (01234) 328164
*Acid-free boxes, folders and
conservation papers and boards.*

Conservation Resources LLC
8000-H Forbes Place, Springfield
Virginia 22151, USA
tel: (800) 634 6932
fax: (703) 321 0629
Extensive catalogue of conservation
materials, archival products, envi-
ronmental control products and
books for the serious collector.

Conservation Resources
(UK) Ltd.
Units 1, 2 & 4 Pony Road
Horspath Industrial Estate
Cowley, Oxfordshire OX4 2RD
England
tel: (01865) 747755
(after hours: (01844) 218277)
fax: (01865) 747035

Gaylord Brothers
PO Box 4901, Syracuse
New York 13221-4901, USA
tel: (800) 448 6160
Preservation storage materials
and conservation supplies for paper,
books, photographic materials
and textiles.

Liberon Waxes
1A Darley Street, Darlinghurst
NSW 2010, Australia

tel (2) 9360 7780
fax: (2) 9360 7798
Complete range of wood finishes
and conservation products.

Meaco Sales & Marketing
The Woodyards
Daux Road Industrial Estate
Billingshurst
West Sussex RH14 9SJ England
tel: (01493) 784455
fax: (01493) 784084
Humidity monitoring and control.

Novatron Ltd.
Unit 34
Southwater Industrial Estate
Horsham
West Sussex RH13 7UD, England
tel: (01403) 733012
fax: (01403) 733311
Environmental monitoring
equipment.

Preservation Equipment Ltd.
Church Road, Shelfanger
Diss, Norfolk IP22 2DG
England
tel: (01379) 651527
fax: (01379) 650582
Materials and preservation
equipment for conservation.

Rankins (Glass) Company Ltd.
The London Glass Centre
24–34 Pearson Street
London E2 8JD, England
tel: (0171) 729 4200
fax: (0171) 729 7135
Specializes in low-reflective,
conservation and fire-resistant
glass products.

G. Ryder & Co. Ltd.
Denbigh Road
Bletchley, Milton Keynes
Bucks MK1 1DG, England
tel: (01908) 375524
Hand-made archival storage boxes.

Talas
586 Broadway
New York NY 10012, USA
tel: (212) 219 0770
fax: (212) 219 0735
Materials for art restorers, conserva-
tors and bookbinders.

Testfabrics Inc.
415 Delaware Avenue, PO Box 26
West Pittston PA 18643, USA
tel: (717) 603 0432
fax: (717) 603 0433
Materials for textile and object con-
servation and picture restoration.

University Products Inc.
517 Main Street, PO Box 101
Holyoke MA 01041, USA
tel: (413) 532 3372 or toll free in
the US (800) 628 1912
website: http://www.universityprod-
ucts.com
Materials for conservation,
restoration and preservation and
display. Books on conservation.
Use this address for orders in the
US, Central and South America,
Africa and Asia.

In Australia, contact:
S. & M. Supply Co. Pty. Ltd.
PO Box 4296
Kingston Act 2604, Australia
tel: (2) 280 6344
fax: (2) 280 4885

Watkins & Doncaster
The Naturalists, PO Box 5
Cranbrook
Kent TN18 5EZ
England
tel: (01580) 753133
fax: (01580) 754054
Display cases, boxes and related
equipment for all types of natural
collections.

DISPLAY UNITS AND MATERIALS

Altuglas
10 rue du Mail
75002 Paris, France
tel: (1) 42 36 38 74
Custom-made Plexiglas table
frames, columns and boxes.

Timothy James Brauer
Studio 303
1081 South Clarkson Street
Denver, Colorado 80209, USA
tel: (303) 871 0609
Furniture-maker who produces
one-off collector's cabinets.

Michel Chevillard
33 rue Ganneron
75018 Paris, France
tel: (1) 43 87 77 83
fax: (1) 42 93 45 30
Furniture restorer and maker
of cabinets in any style.

Colimbus Fan Display Stand
A. Pzel-de Cock Buning
v. Tedingerbrouckstraat 3
NL-2596 PB The Hague
Netherlands
tel/fax: (70) 32 44 921
Acrylic display stands for fans.

Andrew Crawford
Unit BO2, Acton Business Centre
School Road
London NW10 6TD, England
tel/fax: (0181) 961 7066
e-mail: a.crawford1@virgin.net
website: http://business.
virgin.net/a.crawford1
Decorative display boxes to order.

J. & Y. Crossman
Fir Close
Tytherleigh, Axminster
Devon EX13 7BQ, England
tel: (01460) 221152
fax: (01460) 221008
Manufacturers of adhesive plate
hangers for plates, bowls, tiles made
from glass, wood and china, and
small metal objects. The hangers
are invisible.

Dauphin Display Ltd.
PO Box 602
East Oxford OX44 9LU
England
tel: (01865) 343542
fax: (01865) 343307
Over 250 types of transparent stands
and display units.

Evolution
120 Spring Street, New York
NY 10012, USA
tel: (212) 343 1114
Stands and box-frames for natural
history collections.

Farquar's Pty. Ltd.
25 Loftus Street, Bowral
NSW 2576, Australia
tel: (2) 4862 2210
fax: (2) 4861 4877
Traditional furniture-makers
able to produce cabinets.

Galerie 20
Etienne Leroy & Pierre Leroy
288 rue des Pyrénées
75020 Paris, France
tel: (1) 43 66 83 88
Framing, but also custom-made
cases and vitrines for objects.

Paul Gower Furniture
4 Manor Buildings
North Perrott, Crewkerne
Somerset TA18 7ST, England
tel/fax: (01460) 75959
Innovative collector's cabinets
and other furniture.

David Linley Furniture
60 Pimlico Road
London SW1 W8LP, England
tel: (0171) 730 7300
fax: (0171) 730 8869
Frames, easels and wall brackets.

Peter Lloyd
The Old School House
Hallbankgate, Brampton
Cumbria CA8 2NW, England
tel: (016977) 46698
Fine hardwood boxes.

The London Architectural
Salvage & Supply Co. Ltd.
St. Michael's Church
Mark St (off Paul St)
London EC2A 4ER, England
tel: (0171) 739 0448
fax: (0171) 729 6853
Fixtures and fittings, including
cabinets and glass display bottles.

Maxilla & Mandible Ltd.
451–5 Columbus Avenue
New York NY 10024, USA
tel: (212) 724 6173
fax: (212) 721 1073
Display mounts, cases and domes.

Salvo Magazine
18 Ford Village
Berwick-upon-Tweed
Northumberland, England
tel: (01890) 820333
*Ring for details of dealers in
salvaged architectural items, both
in the UK and overseas.*

Tom Schneider Designs
20 Frognal Way, Hampstead
London NW3 6XE, England
tel: (0181) 275 0306
fax: (0181) 441 7440
e-mail: tschdesign@aol.com
*Cabinets, shelves and console tables.
Call for appointments and list of
stockists.*

**Shopkit Designs
(Head Office)**
100 Cecil Street, North Watford
Herts WD2 5AP, England
tel: (01923) 818282

fax: (01923) 231675
*High-tech one-off display units.
Also low-voltage lighting and
suspension systems.*

**Simonart
D. & J. Simons & Sons Ltd.**
122–150 Hackney Road
London E2 7QL, England
tel: (0171) 739 3744
fax: (0171) 739 4452
*All items for framing, mounting
and hanging.*

Simplex Bookcases & Cabinets
Simplex Factory
High Street, Oldland
Bristol BS15 6TA, England
tel: (0117) 932 2279
fax: (0117) 932 8800
*Hand-crafted solid wood shelves
and cabinets.*

Stephenson Blake & Co. Ltd.
199 Upper Allen Street
Sheffield S3 7GW, England
tel: (0114) 272 8325
fax: (0114) 272 0065
Custom-made display cabinets.

Stockman London Ltd.
Stockman House
9 Dallington Street
London EC1V OBQ, England
tel: (0171) 251 6943
fax: (0171) 250 1798
*Suppliers of display torsos covered in
cream cotton jersey for costumes.*

**Andy Thornton Architectural
Antiques**
Ainleys Industrial Estate
Elland, Halifax
West Yorkshire HX5 9JP, England
tel: (01422) 375595
*Reclaimed architectural and
interior fittings.*

Patrick Vastel
143 rue du Général-Leclerc
50110 Tourlaville
Cherbourg, France
tel: (2) 33 22 46 07
fax: (2) 33 22 96 29
*Restorer of marquetry for clients
worldwide, cabinetmaker.*

Vitrines Vendome
81 rue des Archieves
75003 Paris, France
tel: (1) 42 72 58 38
fax: (1) 42 72 65 59
*High-quality cabinets for collectors
and museums.*

Walcot Reclamation
108 Walcot Street
Bath, England
tel: (01225) 444404
Cupboards, shelving and cabinets.

INSTALLERS AND FRAMERS

Academy Framing
Royal Academy of Arts
Burlington House
London W1V ODS, England
tel: (0171) 300 5646
fax: (0171) 300 8001
*Restoration of frames, re-gilding
of frames, mirrors and framing.*

**Amyas Naegele
Fine Art Bases Ltd.**
347 West 36th Street, 16th Floor
New York NY 10018, USA
tel/fax: (212) 465 0524
Specialist base-maker.

La Baguette de Bois
44 rue Lepic, 75018 Paris, France
tel: (1) 46 06 36 80
fax: (1) 42 54 54 92
Antique and modern frames.

Benchmark
PO Box 214
Rosemont NJ 08556, USA
tel: (609) 397 1131
fax: (609) 397 1159

Benchmark
Ryder Museums & Galleries
1 Red Deer Court
Elm Road, Winchester
Hampshire SO22 5AG, England
tel: (01962) 841913
fax: (01962) 841923
e-mail: ryder @easynet.co.uk
*Provides custom mount-making and
installation services.*

Bourlet Fine Art Framers
32 Connaught Street
London W2 2AY
England
tel/fax: (0171) 724 4837
e-mail: frames@bourlet.co.uk
*Fine-art framers, gilders and
restorers. Offer a scanning service
to help with the selection of frames
and mounts.*

Colin Bowles Ltd.
Unit 15
Heliport Estate
Bridges Court
London SW11 3RE
England
tel: (0171) 228 5139
fax: (0171) 738 2559
*Mounts for antiquities and works
of art.*

Charlotte
9 cité Dupetit-Thouars
75003 Paris, France
tel: (1) 42 77 85 15
fax: (1) 42 77 85 80
*Framers of watercolours, gouaches,
engravings, lithographs, canvases
and tapestries.*

Claude Galatry
43 rue de la Gare de Reuilly
75012 Paris, France
tel: (1) 43 07 24 92
*All types of frames, especially
for miniatures in round and
oval shapes.*

The Hangman
7–17 Ithaca Road
Elizabeth Bay, Sydney
NSW 2011, Australia
tel: (2) 9368 0608
*Picture hanging for private
collectors.*

Charles Hewitt
30 Queen Street, Woollahra,
Sydney, NSW 2025, Australia
tel: (2) 9327 8185
fax: (2) 9699 1480
*Gilding, art restoration and
picture hanging services.*

Walter McLaren
2 Churchfields, Horsell Park
Woking GU21 4LX, England
tel: (01483) 772299 or 772896
fax: (01483) 730254
Framing service for fans.

McWhinne and Green
43 William Street
Paddington, Sydney
NSW 2021, Australia
tel: (2) 9331 7073
Mounter and base-maker.

Paul Mitchell Ltd.
99 New Bond Street
London W1Y 9L, England
tel: (0171) 493 8732
fax: (0171) 409 7136
*Specialists in framing and conserv-
ing period and contemporary paintings and drawings.*

Paddington Frames
18 Queen Street
Chippendale
Sydney
NSW 2008, Australia
tel/fax: (2) 9319 3193
Framing, restoration and mounting.

The Paris American Art Co.
4 rue Bonaparte
75006 Paris, France
tel: (1) 43 26 09 93
fax: (1) 43 54 33 80
*Framing in all styles, including
frames for mirrors and miniatures.*

Ronayne Design
17 Manor Avenue
London SE4 IPE
England
tel: (0181) 692 8950
fax: (0181) 692 4345
*Primarily a museum and exhibition
designer, but undertakes some
private work.*

Ross Skelton
47 Dundalk Road
London SE4 2JJ, England
tel: (0171) 639 0359
Suppliers of mounts of all types.

LIGHTING SUPPLIERS AND DESIGNERS

**Drs William Allen
& Stephen Cannon-Brookes**
Bickerdike Allen Partners
121 Salusbury Road
London NW6 6RG, England
tel: (0171) 625 4411
fax: (0171) 625 0250
*Lighting consultants to museums
and private collectors.*

Atelier Christian de Beaumont
11 rue Frederic Sauton
75005 Paris, France
tel: (1) 43 29 88 75
fax: (1) 40 51 88 06
Lighting for decorative collectables.

Concord Lighting Ltd.
174 High Holborn
London WC1V 7AA, England
tel: (0171) 497 1400
fax: (0171) 497 1404
export office:
tel: (01273) 515811
fax: (01273) 512688
*Offers a complete range of fixtures
and lamps for all needs.*

John Cullen Lighting
585 King's Road
London SW6 2EH, England
tel: (0171) 371 5400
*Consultants in lighting effects
with an exculsive range of
products.*

Elsec
Littlemore Scientific Engineering
Railway Lane
Littlemore
Oxford OX4 4PZ, England
tel: (01865) 747437
fax: (01865) 747780
e-mail: sales @ elsec.co.uk
UV and light monitors.

Hanwell Instruments
PO Box 54
East Norwich
NY 11732, USA
tel: (800) 800 0588/
(516) 624 2900
fax: (516) 624 9363
*Monitoring equipment for lights,
temperature and relative humidity.*

**The Lighting Services
Partnership**
Myrtle House
Headcorn Road, Grafty Green
Kent ME17 2AR, England
tel/fax: (01622) 850381
e-mail: lightserv1@aol.com
Fine-art lighting specialist.

Lighting Services Inc.
2 Kay Fries Drive
Stony Point NY 10980, USA
tel: (800) 999 9574
or (914) 942 2800
fax: (914) 942 2177
website: http:///www.Lighting
ServicesInc.com
*Specialist manufacturers for
museum environments.*

Light Projects Ltd.
23 Jacob Street
London SW1 2BG, England
tel: (0171) 231 8282
fax: (0171) 237 4342
*Architectural and display lighting
using low-voltage lighting fixtures.*

Modaluce
1 Greville Street, Clovelly
Sydney, NSW 2031, Australia
tel: (2) 9664 2193
fax: (2) 9664 2176
Lighting for collectors.

Pinpoint Fibreoptics Ltd.
PO Box 7085
Beverly Hills CA 90212, USA
tel: (310) 276 3437
fax: (310) 276 3475
Leading supplier of fibre optics.

SUN-X (UK) Ltd.
Madeira Parade, Bognor Regis
West Sussex PO22 8DX, England
tel: (01243) 826441
fax: (01243) 829691
e-mail: sun-x@argonet.co.uk
Filters and sun-blinds.

Westgate Solar Control
PO Box 21, Bellasis Street
Stafford ST16 3YJ, England
tel: (01785) 242181
UV and heat filters.

SECURITY

Art & Antiques Squad
New Scotland Yard
confidential tel: (0171) 230 4974

*To help authorities fight the trade in
stolen works of art, an international
standard for describing artefacts has
been drawn up by 84 countries
under the direction of the Getty
Information Institute. The Object ID
has been adopted by Interpol,
Unesco, the Council of Europe, the
FBI, New Scotland Yard, the British
Museum and the Art Loss Register
among others. Available from The
Getty Information Institute or the
offices of the Art Loss Register.*

Art Loss Register
12 Grosvenor Place
London SW1X 7HH,
England
tel: (0171) 235 3393
fax: (0171) 235 1652
e-mail: artloss@artloss.co.uk
website: www.artloss.com

Art Loss Register
666 Fifth Avenue, 21st Floor
New York NY 10103, USA
tel: (212) 262 4831
fax: (212) 262 4831
e-mail: alrnewyork@aol.com
website: www.artloss.com

Art Loss Register
Poststrasse 7
40213 Düsseldorf, Germany
tel: (211) 138 0646
fax: (211) 323 6830
e-mail: artloss@artloss.com
website: www.artloss.com

Art Loss Register
The Getty Information Institute
1200 Getty Center Drive
Suite 3000 Los Angeles
CA 90049-1681, USA
fax: (310) 440 7715
website: www.gii.getty.edu/pco

The Loss Register
1060 Hay Street, PO Box 589
West Perth 6872, Western Australia
tel: (9) 495 4040
fax: (9) 495 4060
e-mail: admin@lossreg.com.u
website: Admin@lossreg.com.u

**Association of Fine Art
Photographers**
Minton, Monkmead Copse
West Chiltington, Pulborough
West Sussex RH20 2PD, England
tel: (01798) 813293
*Maintains a register of security-
cleared photographers who specialize
in photographing fine art objects.
Some of the members are listed here:*

Kenneth Anderson
37 Hillview Avenue, Newtonabbey
County Antrim BT36 6AF
Northern Ireland
tel: (01232) 862642

P.J. Gates Photography Ltd.
94 New Bond Street
London W1Y 9LA, England
tel: (0171) 629 4962
fax: (0171) 493 4324

Joris Luyten
Veltwycklaan 84, B-2180 Ekeren
Antwerp, Belgium
tel: (3) 544 9999
fax: (3) 544 9775

Michael Pugh
Incorporated Photographer
14 East Rise, Llanisben
Cardiff CP4 5RJ, Wales
tel: (01222) 751368

Kenneth Smith
6 Lussielaw Road
Edinburgh
Lothian EH9 3BX, Scotland
tel: (0131) 667 6159

R. & S. Brooks
15 Halcyon Avenue, Wahroonga
NSW 2076, Australia
tel: (2) 9489 7843

**International Foundation
for Art Research (IFAR)**
Suite 1234, 500 5th Avenue
New York, NY 10110, USA
tel: (212) 391 6234
fax: (212) 391 8794
*Established in 1977 it regularly
publishes stolen works of art in partnership with the Art Loss Register,
a database of stolen and missing
works of art operating as a commercial venture from offices in London,
New York, Perth, Düsseldorf and
St Petersburg. It acts as a clearing
house for information on stolen art,
assisting law enforcement agencies,
insurers, dealers and collectors
in the battle against art theft. They
also have representatives in Dublin
and Stockholm.*

SmartWater Europe Ltd.
PO Box 23, Newport
Shropshire TF10 7UX, England
tel: (01952) 222706
fax: (01952) 641150
website: http://www.smartwater.com
*SmartWater is a harmless solution
which after application leaves a
permanent chemically coded
'fingerprint'. It is the only crime pre-
vention product made under licence
by the Forensic Science Service, a
UK Government Executive Agency.*

Trace Publications Ltd.
Mill Court, Furrlongs, Newport
Isle of Wight PO30 2AA, England
tel: (01983) 826000
fax: (01983) 826201
e-mail: trace@thesaurus.co.uk
website: http://www.trace.co.uk
*Monthly magazine which describes
and illustrates stolen and missing
fine art. Distributed internationally
to police and art dealers.*

Thesaurus Group Ltd.
76 Gloucester Place
London W1H 4DQ, England
tel: (0171) 487 3401
fax: (0171) 487 4211
e-mail: sales@thesaurus.co.uk
website: http://www.thesaurus.co.uk
*The world's largest processor of
auction house information. The
operation, owned by Trace
magazine under the Thesaurus
Group Company, uses its extensive
access to information of auction
activity to recover objects.*

*For insurance brokers and security
consulting firms that specialize in
fine art insurance and security it is*

*best to contact the art and antique
associations in your country or
local museums for lists of approved
companies or national organizations
for security and insurance companies. Several are listed below:*

BRA Australia Pty. Ltd.
256 Queen Street, Melbourne
Victoria 3000, Australia
tel: (3) 9670 9341
fax: (3) 9670 2841
e-mail: bra@bra-aust.com.au
*Insurance brokers to Australian
Antique Dealers Association members, agent in Australia for Houlder
Insurance Services International Ltd.*

Graphic Park Ltd.
Hobson House, 155 Gower Street
London WC1E 6BJ, England
tel: (0171) 388 6060
fax: (0171) 388 6622
e-mail: docutga@dial.pipex.com
*A software package called Romulus
which will print off high-quality
pictures and play video-images on a
PC. Used by dealers and collectors
to record images of their objects for
security and sales purposes.*

**Micro Photographic
Fingerprinting**
PO Box 1019
Newcastle-under-Lyme
Staffordshire ST5 5TB, England
tel: (01782) 740 780
fax: (01782) 740 790
*A micro-image profile is carried
out without marking or making
any impression on objects, thus
producing a completely unique
recording. The process cannot be
detected by a criminal using UV
lights or scanners.*

**The National Approval
Council for Security Systems
(NACOSS)**
Queensgate House
14 Cookham Road
Berkshire SL6 8AJ, England
tel: (01628) 637512
fax: (01628) 773367
e-mail: nacoss@nacoss.org
website: http://www.nacoss.org
*Regulates and approves security
companies involved in the installation of security systems.*

**Nordstern Insurance
Companies**
78 Leadenhall Street
London EC3A 3DH, England
tel: (0171) 626 5001
fax: (0171) 626 4606
USA: tel: (212) 412 0700
fax: (212) 412 0820
Germany: tel: (221) 148 4653
fax: (221) 148 4655
*Provide insurance for private
collectors worldwide with offices
in Europe and the United States.*

BIBLIOGRAPHY

We would like to thank the authors of the following works which provided an invaluable source of reference in the writing of the book.

Allen, W. 'Lighting Fine Paintings'
in *The Picture Restorer*
(No 11, Spring 1997, pp. 11–13)

Ayers, J., Impey, O. & Mallet, J.V.G.
Porcelain for Palaces (London:
Oriental Ceramic Society, 1990)

Belk, Russell W. *Collecting in a
Consumer Society* (London & New
York: Routledge, 1995)

Brace, Marianne 'Living in a
Material World' in *An Independent
Eye* (February 17, 1998, pp. 2–3)

Elsner, J. & Cardinal, R., eds.
The Cultures of Collecting
(London: Reaktion Books, 1994)

Gaillemin, Jean-Louis
'Oranienbaum: The Meissen Room'
in *The World of Interiors*
(Vol 14, no 12, 1994, pp. 62–5)

Impey, O. & MacGregor, A., eds.
The Origins of Museums
(Oxford: Clarendon Press, 1985)

Jackson-Stops, Gervase, ed.
The Treasure Houses of Britain
(New Haven & London: Yale
University Press, 1985)

Katz, Sylvia *Classic Plastics from
Bakelite to High-Tech* (London:
Thames & Hudson, 1984)

Le Pelley, Nicolette 'Chevening'
in *The World of Interiors*
(Vol 14, no 9, 1994, pp. 74–7)

Lichter, Gerhard *Fossil Collector's
Handbook* (New York: Sterling
Publishing Co., 1993)

MacGregor, A., ed. *Sir Hans
Sloane* (London: British Museum
Press, 1994)

Norman, Geraldine 'Life with
Picasso' in *Independent on Sunday*
(September, 28 1997, pp. 16–9)

Parnell, Geoffrey 'The King's Guard
Chamber' in *Apollo* (August 1994,
pp. 60–4)

Pearce, Susan M., ed. *Interpreting
Objects and Collections* (London &
New York: Routledge, 1994)

Pearce, Susan M. *On Collecting*
(London & New York: Routledge,
1995)

Price, D. 'John Woodward and
a surviving British geological
collection from the early eighteenth

century' in *Journal of the History
of Collections* (Vol 1, No 1, 1989,
pp. 79–95)

Purcell, R.W. & Gould, S.J. *Finders,
Keepers* (London: Hutchinson
Radius, 1992)

Sale, Jonathan 'Paper Values' in
Independent on Sunday
(February 8, 1998, pp. 56–7)

Scheicher, E. 'Historiography and
display: The 'Heldenrüstkammer'
of Archduke Ferdinand II in
Schloss Ambras' in *Journal of
the History of Collections*
(Vol 2, no 1, 1990, pp. 69–79)

Schultz, A., ed. *Caring for your
Collections* (New York: Harry N.
Abrams, Inc., 1992)

Shulsky, L.R. 'Kensington and de
Voorst: two porcelain collections' in
Journal of the History of Collections
(Vol 2, no 1, 1990, pp. 47–62)

Simon, Jacob *The Art of the
Picture Frame: Artists, Patrons
and the Framing of Portraits in
Britain* (London: National Portrait
Gallery, 1996)

Stansfield, G. & Mathias, J. *Manual
of Natural History Curatorship*
(London: HMSO Publications, 1994)

Sturges, Fiona 'Yin, Yang and Yen'
in *Independent on Sunday*
(January 11, 1998, pp. 19–20)

Thornton, P. & Dorey, H.
*A Miscellany of Objects from Sir
John Soane's Museum* (London:
Laurence King, 1992)

Vollmer, J.E., Keall, E.J. & Nagai-
Berthrong, E. *Silk Roads – China
Ships* (Toronto: The Royal Ontario
Museum, 1983)

von Habsburg, Géza *Princely
Treasures* (London: Thames &
Hudson Ltd., 1997)

Waterfield, G., ed. *Palaces of Art:
Art Galleries in Britain 1790–1990*
(London: Dulwich Picture
Gallery, 1991)

Wilton, A. & Bignamini, I., eds.
Grand Tour (London: Tate Gallery
Publishing, 1996)

Windsor, John 'Learn To Play Your
Cards Right' in *Independent on
Sunday* (October 15, 1995, pp. 80–1)

Numbers in *italics* refer
to illustration captions

Previous page: *The white walls of
this elegant room provide the
perfect backdrop for a collection
of blue-and-white porcelain. The
five rows of consoles have been
cleverly staggered across the wall,
while the mirror has been angled
to echo the shapes of the vases,
adding the depth and reflected
light that contribute to the
grandeur of this composition.*

Conran Octopus would like to thank the following photographers and organizations for their kind permission to reproduce the photographs in this book:

4–5 Paul Ryan/International Interiors (Stamberg & Aferiat Architects); 6 Marie-Pierre Morel (G. Lesigne); 8 Tom Leighton/The World of Interiors; 11 © The National Gallery, London; 12 Elke Walford, Courtesy of The Hamburger Kunsthalle; 13 left The British Museum; 13 right The Dean & Chapter of Canterbury; 14 The British Library; 15 above The Ashmolean Museum, Oxford; 15 below The British Library; 16–17 The Natural History Museum, London; 18 Richard Bryant/Arcaid; 19 The British Museum; 20 left Sotheby's; 20 right Courtesy of the Pennsylvania Academy of the Fine Arts, Philadelphia (gift of Mrs Sarah Harrison, The Joseph Harrison Jr collection); 21 The Pitt-Rivers Museum, University of Oxford; 22 Rosamond Wolff Purcell; 23 The National Trust Photographic Library/John Hammond; 24 C. Simon Sykes/The Interior Archive; 25 above The Royal College of Surgeons of England; 25 below © The Saatchi Collection, London; 26 Collection Hui Bon Hoa/Pascal Hinous/Agence Top; 28 Robin Matthews; 29 Tim Beddow/The World of Interiors; 30 Collection McAlpine/Pascal Hinous/Agence Top; 31 Collection Macaire/Pascal Hinous/ Agence Top; 32–33 The Freud Museum, London; 34 Allen Jones; 35 C. Simon Sykes/The Interior Archive; 36 Alan Weintraub/Arcaid; 37 above Tim Beddow/Elizabeth Whiting & Associates; 37 below Rosamond Wolff Purcell; 38 Marie-Pierre Morel (Moni Linz); 39 Dook (Eric Falconer); 40 Gil Michael/Elvis Presley Enterprises; 41 Guitars courtesy of The Chinery Collection; 42 Dennis Stone/Elizabeth Whiting & Associates (James Bunce); 43 Annet Held/Arcaid; 44 Fritz von der Schulenburg/The Interior Archive; 47 Fritz von der Schulenburg/The Interior Archive (Jorg Marguard); 48 left Historic Royal Palaces; 48 right Fritz von der Schulenburg/The World of Interiors; 49 Fritz von der Schulenburg/The World of Interiors; 50 C. Simon Sykes/The Interior Archive; 51 The Royal Danish Collections, Rosenborg; 52 Fritz von der Schulenburg/The Interior Archive; 53 C. Simon Sykes/The Interior Archive; 54 James Mortimer/The World of Interiors; 55 Fritz von der Schulenburg/The Interior Archive (Bill Blass); 56 Alberto Piovano/Arcaid (Architect: Chris Mys); 57 Oberto Gili/Condé Nast; 58 left Richard Bryant/Arcaid (Architect: Arato Isozaki); 58 right C. Simon Sykes/The Interior Archive; 59 C. Simon Sykes/The Interior Archive (Candida Lycett-Green); 60 James Mortimer/The World of Interiors; 61 Simon Upton/The Interior Archive; 62 above left Joshua Greene; 62 above right Pascal Chevalier/The World of Interiors; 62 below right and 63 Tim Beddow/The World of Interiors; 64 Fritz von der Schulenburg/The Interior Archive (Kath Kidston); 65 C. Simon Sykes/The Interior Archive (Jane Stubbs); 66 left Grazia Branco/Iketrade; 66 right Fritz von der Schulenburg/The Interior Archive (Jacques Grange); 67 Oberto Gili/Town & Country (Mr & Mrs Pennoyer); 68 James Mortimer/The World of Interiors; 69 Peo Eriksson/Camera Press; 70

Jean-Francois Jaussaud/The World of Interiors; 71 Richard Bryant/Arcaid (Architect: Tsao McKown); 72 left Jacques Dirand/The Interior Archive; 72 right Jacques Dirand/The Interior Archive (Henry Moore); 73 Mark Darly/Esto Photographics; 74 Deidi von Schaewen (Mr Zecca); 75 Deidi von Schaewen (Mr & Mrs Sattler); 76–77 C. Simon Sykes/The Interior Archive; 78 left James Mortimer/The Interior Archive (Christopher Hodsell); 78 right Deidi von Schaewen; 79 Fritz von der Schulenburg/The Interior Archive; 80 Alexander van Berge; 81 Deidi von Schaewen (Jacques Garcia); 82 Richard Bryant/Arcaid (Apartment Robert Hutchinson); 83 Ray Main/Mainstream; 84 Tim Street Porter/Elizabeth Whiting & Associates; 85 above Peter Aprahamian (Peter Adler); 85 below Deidi von Schaewen (Mr & Mrs Dubois la Chartre); 86 Deidi von Schaewen (Mr & Mrs Nahon); 87 William Abranowicz/Art & Commerce Anthology Inc (Mr & Mrs Mendelson); 88 Fritz von der Schulenburg/The Interior Archive; 89–90 left James Mortimer/The World of Interiors; 90 right Hotze Eisma; 91 Peter Aprahamian (Jenny Bolton); 92 Deidi von Schaewen; 93 Simon Upton/The World of Interiors; 94 Tim Clinch © House & Garden/Conde Nast; 95 Alan Weintraub/Arcaid; 96 Scott Frances/Esto Photographics; 97 left Jaques Dirand/The Interior Archive (Chantal Chenel); 97 right Wulf Brackrock; 98 C. Simon Sykes © House & Garden/Condé Nast; 99 above Paul Ryan/International Interiors (Designer: Mark Rossi); 99 below Fritz von der Schulenburg/The Interior Archive; 100 Henry Wilson/The Interior Archive (Mibus); 101 Verne Fotografie (Miller Apartment, New York); 102 Eric Morin/The World of Interiors; 103 Fritz von der Schulenburg/The Interior Archive; 104 left Tim Goffe/The Interior Archive; 104 right Camera Press; 105 Fritz von der Schulenburg/The Interior Archive (Axel Verwoordt); 106 Fritz von der Schulenburg/The Interior Archive (John Russell); 107 C. Simon Sykes/The Interior Archive (Therese and Erwin Harris); 108 Ray Main/Mainstream; 109 Earl Carter/Belle/Arcaid; 110 Gilles de Chabeneix/Marie Claire Maison; 111 Earl Carter/Belle/Arcaid; 112 Fritz von der Schulenburg/The Interior Archive; 113 Max Forsythe/The World of Interiors; 114 Paul Ryan/International Interiors (Designer: George Beylerian); 115 Denis Krukowski/The World of Interiors; 116 Christian Sarramon (Anne and Alois Rosat); 117 above Alan Weintraub/Arcaid; 117 below Fritz von der Schulenburg/The Interior Archive (Jorg Marguard); 118 Scott Frances/Esto Photographics; 119 Richard Davies/The World of Interiors; 120 William Abranowicz/Art & Commerce Anthology Inc (Mr & Mrs Mendelson); 121 Joshua Greene; 122 Collection J.C. Farhi/Pascal Hinous/Agence Top; 123 Tim Street Porter/Elizabeth Whiting Associates; 124 left Ray Main/Mainstream; 124 right Elizabeth Whiting & Associates; 125 Oberto Gili/ Courtesy of House & Garden, © 1992 by The Condé Nast Publications Inc; 126 Fritz von der Schulenburg/The Interior Archive (John Stefanidis); 129 Marie-Pierre Morel/Daniel Rozensztroch/Marie Claire Maison; 130 Fritz von der Schulenburg/The Interior Archive (Laura

Biagiotti); 132 Courtesy of The National Portrait Gallery, London; 133 Mirjam Bleeker/Production Frank Visser/Taverne Agency; 134 Pieter Estersohn/LachaPelle Representation (Stuart Parr); 135 below Peo Eriksson/Camera Press; 139 above Jean Pierre Godeaut (Arman Home); 139 below Deidi von Schaewen (Mr Lefur); 140 left Ray Main/Mainstream; 140 right Paul Rocheleau; 141 Alberto Piovano/Arcaid (Architect: Chris Mys); 143 left Christian Sarramon; 143 right Paul Rocheleau (The Jerome and Selma Blum Private Collection); 146 left Simon Brown/Camera Press; 146 right Fritz von der Schulenburg/The Interior Archive; 147 Mirjam Bleeker/Production Frank Visser/Taverne Agency; 148 Simon McBride; 149 Camera Press; 151 Joshua Greene; 160 Arnaud Carpentier; 163–165 Rosamond Wolff Purcell; 166–168 English Heritage Photographic Library; 169 The Textile Conservation Centre; 171 Elizabeth Whiting & Associates; 172 The Ancient Art & Architecture Collection; 173 Joshua Greene; 174 The National Trust Photographic Library; 175 Simon Brown/The Interior Archive; 176 The National Trust Photographic Library; 177 Geo Science Features Picture Library; 178 The Sylvia Katz Collection; 187 Fritz von der Schulenburg/The World of Interiors

The following photographs were taken specially for Conran Octopus by Simon Upton and styled by Cynthia Inions: Pages 2–3 (Guinevere Antiques, London); 131 (John Soane's Museum); 135 above (Julia Boston), 136–137 (Antiques, London); 138 ('Sandy Hay' by Etienne Millner); 142 left (Guinevere Antiques, London); 142 right (Antiques, London); 144 (Ceramics: Lucie Rie); 145 (Ceramics: Keith Skeel); 152–153 (Stylist: Joan Hecktermann); 154 above (Pep Sala); 154 below (Vitra), 155 above left (Themes & Variations, London); 155 above right (Kenji Yazaki sculptures courtesy of Twentieth Century Design); 155 below left (The David Gill Gallery, London); 155 below right (Hemisphere, London); 156–159 (Jonathan Adler 'Couture' ceramics from Space)

Every effort has been made to trace the copyright holders. We apologize in advance for any unintentional omission, and would be pleased to insert the appropriate acknowledgement in any subsequent edition.

Author's acknowledgements

We would like to thank the following for their assistance and expert advice: Drs William Allen & Stephen Cannon-Brookes, lighting consultants for Bickerdike Allen Partners; Brian Beacock, Treasurer of the British Teddy Bear Association; Errol Fuller, author and expert on rare and extinct birds; Allan Gordon of The Doll's Hospital; Joan Hecktermann, former art director at *World of Interiors* who helped enormously in the initial picture selection; Sylvia Katz, author and authority on plastics; Walter McLaren, framer and collector of fans; Amyas Naegele, New York mount-maker; Lord Palumbo, an eclectic English collector; and Geoffrey Parnell, Keeper of Tower History at the Tower of London.